C.F. Martin & Co.
EST. 1833

MARTIN GUITAR
MASTERPIECES

A SHOWCASE OF ARTISTS' EDITIONS, LIMITED EDITIONS, AND CUSTOM GUITARS

MARTIN GUITAR
MASTERPIECES

A SHOWCASE OF ARTISTS' EDITIONS, LIMITED EDITIONS, AND CUSTOM GUITARS

DICK BOAK   INTRODUCTION BY C. F. MARTIN IV   FOREWORD BY STEVE MILLER

BULFINCH PRESS   AOL TIME WARNER BOOK GROUP   BOSTON · NEW YORK · LONDON

DEDICATION

TO THE ARTISTS WHOM I HAVE HAD THE GREAT HONOR OF WORKING WITH ON MANY OF THESE SPECIAL
GUITARS, AND TO ALL OF THE PEOPLE THAT OWN, LOVE AND PLAY MARTIN GUITARS.
WITHOUT YOU, THESE WONDERFUL TOOLS ARE JUST WOODEN BOXES WITH SOME TAUT WIRE ATTACHED.

THANKS:

TO SUSAN, EMILY AND GRACE FOR THEIR PATIENCE WITH ME.
TO COHORTS DAVID COSTA AND COLIN WEBB, WITHOUT WHOM THIS BOOK WOULD NEVER HAVE HAPPENED.
TO ALL OF MY CO-WORKERS AT MARTIN FOR BRINGING THESE INSTRUMENTS TO FRUITION.
TO CHRIS MARTIN FOR HIS YEARS OF FRIENDSHIP AND SUPPORT.
TO RONNIE LIPPIN, BILL BUSH, MARSHALL NEWMAN AND DIANE PONZIO FOR THEIR RESEARCH
AND SOUNDING BOARD TEXT ASSISTANCE.
TO LARRY SIFEL, JEFF HARDING AND ALL OF THE GREAT FOLKS AT PEARLWORKS.
TO MY TALENTED FRIEND DAVID NICHOLS OF CUSTOM PEARL INLAY.
TO THE INCREDIBLE INLAY ARTISTRY OF LARRY ROBINSON.
TO THE GREAT TALENT AND KINSHIP OF JOHN STERLING RUTH, WHOSE MANY PHOTOGRAPHS GRACE THIS BOOK,
AND TO HIS ASSISTANT ERIK NELSON.
TO MICHAEL L. SAND FOR HIS SUPPORT AND ENTHUSIASM.

Created and produced by
Palazzo Editions Ltd
15 Gay Street, Bath, BA1 2PH

Art direction and design by
David Costa and Emil Dacany for Wherefore Art?
Primrose Hill, London

Text copyright © Dick Boak

Typeset in Garamond & Trajan

First Edition

ISBN 0-8212-2835-8

Library of Congress Control Number 2003101537

Bulfinch Press is a division of AOL Time Warner Book Group.

PRINTED IN SINGAPORE

CONTENTS

FOREWORD BY STEVE MILLER

WHEN I WAS A CHILD we had musicians and musical instruments in our home all the time. It was in the late forties — Les Paul and Mary Ford were putting their act together at a club in the neighborhood and were regular visitors to our home along with Tal Farlow, Charles Mingus, Red Norvo, and many others. My Uncle Paul had played violin in the Paul Whiteman Orchestra, my Uncle Dale was a guitar player and my mom sang jazz. My dad, a physician, was a tape-recorder nut and recorded everything so I was surrounded by musicians, technology, guitars, and tape recorders.

I will never forget the day my Uncle Dale came by with his guitar, let me strum it and take it to my room by myself to play with it. I was four years old and in love with Mary Ford and wanted nothing more than to become a guitar player just like Les Paul. The next morning my uncle left very early. I went running downstairs and looked behind the couch to see if the guitar was still there and it was! I opened the case, looked at the purple velvet lining and reached down to touch the beautiful guitar inside. I fell in love with my first instrument and my heart almost burst with gratitude.

Years later, as I mull over a lifetime spent playing and collecting guitars, and considering all the people who have inspired me to play and to love the instrument, people like Les Paul and T Bone Walker, Freddy King and Jimmy Reed and Otis Rush, one person stands out among them all as the one who taught me the most about the actual instrument. That person is Dick Boak. It was Dick who introduced me to the world of luthiers — the people who actually make the instruments.

After years of buying instruments in stores I had finally gotten to the point of wanting to have a custom guitar built. A friend gave me Dick's name and number and I called him to ask for his advice. He invited me to visit him at the Martin factory and as I was in the neighborhood, I headed the tour bus to Nazareth and thus started an adventure that is ongoing.

Dick took me through the factory to see how the instruments were being made and then showed me his collection of personal guitars. We became friends and he quickly introduced me to several great guitar builders. He became my source of information for everything. He knew everyone: the best archtop builders, the best electric-guitar builders, and many great acoustic players. He showed me where to get the best wood, and who to go to for specialized design work. I soon realized I had found the motherlode of all guitar information, but it went even further than that.

Dick and some friends had founded ASIA, the Association of Stringed Instrument Artisans, a group of more than two thousand instrument makers from around the world that had been joined together through years of hard work. He was writing, editing, and publishing a journal called *Guitarmaker* that dealt with all aspects of instrument making and was spending an ungodly amount of time on ASIA with the intention of bringing a sense of cohesiveness and information sharing to the guitarmaking craft. And this was in his spare time! During work hours he was fully immersed in advertising, publicity, newsletters, instrument design, artist relations, and eventually the collaborative signature-model projects that make up a good portion of this book.

As you go through these pages and marvel at the beauty of these guitars you should know that even though he might understate his role, Dick has played a significant part in the designs of many of the artist models shown here. It is projects like these that have challenged the artistry and talent of the Martin craftspeople to new heights. This remarkable collection of instruments reflects the knowledge, craftsmanship, and commitment to excellence that has maintained Martin's position as America's premier maker of acoustic guitars.

It is equally clear from many of the commemorative and milestone guitars designed or initiated by Chris Martin that he is truly an inspired leader and a very significant creative force within the company. This is most unusual for a CEO. I personally commend Chris for allowing his fellow employees the latitude to honor all of these artists and to bring these beautiful instruments to fruition.

The best part of all is that many of these great instruments, although rare, can actually be acquired and enjoyed. I certainly have! I've written some of my best songs with my Martin guitars and mysteriously, my Martin collection continues to grow. It goes without saying that I'm very proud to have been personally honored with my own signature model.

Thank you, Dick and Chris and all the great people at Martin, for sharing your art with the world. I am sure that many of the beautiful instruments shown in these pages are destined to become museum pieces, but frankly, I plan to play the finish off mine!

Steve Miller

Steve Miller
(aka Maurice, the Gangster of Love, the Joker, the Space Cowboy, etc.)
January 31, 2003 — Somewhere in Idaho

INTRODUCTION BY C. F. MARTIN IV

LOOKING THROUGH THIS BOOK as it was beginning to grow, my first reaction was that I hadn't realized how many of these very special guitars we were able to develop and produce in such a relatively short space of time — especially since, in all honesty, we owe much of the success of this program to chance.

The history of our company is certainly well known and widely documented, so I don't need to retell that story here. The incredible legacy passed on to me from my predecessors was relatively intact, though there were some rocky times during the seventies and early eighties. We got through it, however, and unlike many of the other companies in our business, avoided any endorsement arrangements. We simply assumed that if we built "a better mousetrap," the world would beat a path to our door. In effect that's what happened. Most of the serious musicians were playing Martin guitars because they were, quite simply, the best available tools of the trade.

Our first real artist collaboration, during my tenure as Chairman and CEO of the company, paid tribute to the late Perry Bechtel, a popular plectrum banjo and guitar player of the twenties and thirties era. To any guitar enthusiast, Perry's influence on Martin's development of the 14-fret neck requires little explanation. Ken Cagle, our district sales manager from Atlanta, Georgia, had established contact with Perry's widow and, with her cooperation, we were successful in developing the OM-28PB Commemorative Edition. This project allayed some of my doubts about embarking on anything similar, although the topic still remained controversial from the standpoint of our dealers.

But shortly after the Bechtel model hit the market, a long-standing and nagging curiosity of mine to seek out the first D-45 took me to the Gene Autry Museum of Western Heritage in Los Angeles. I was tremendously impressed with the place — far beyond The Singing Cowboy and memorabilia of the Hollywood cowboy experience, fine sculptures, paintings, and exhibits covered a comprehensive history of the West and, of course, Gene's glass-encased 12-fret D-45, lacking a bridge pin or two, justified each of the three thousand miles or so it took to get to see it. But it was at the exit, through the museum shop with its reproduction Gene Autry lunchboxes and penknives, that the idea came into my head — why not a reproduction Gene Autry guitar? It was an ambitious concept, and in trepidation of making a deal with a movie and recording legend who owned a museum, a radio station, and a baseball team, I grasped at the concept of offering not only a recreation of Gene's famous guitar but also a donation to the museum, a nonprofit charity, in the form of a royalty on each instrument sold. Gene loved the idea and the resulting deal initiated our first Signature Edition with a living artist. It also brought a magnificent instrument to the market and gave us an excellent template for future signature-model collaborations.

Some really great designs have emerged through the special relationships that we have nourished with our celebrity artists. Players and enthusiasts worldwide love the resulting products, and the staff and employees here at Martin flourish at the challenge of working with demanding specifications and materials of the very highest quality. On top of all that, these collaborations have enabled us to claim, and sometimes to recapture, the musical heritage that deservedly belongs to us.

Hand-craftsmanship and technology continue to be blended into the company culture as they always have been — without either, Martin guitars would not be as prevalent or as acclaimed as they are today. It shouldn't be any surprise that the special guitars included within these pages reflect change and constancy, history and innovation. They are a celebration of everything that makes the Martin tradition worthy of being preserved. When future generations look back at what we have done, I want them to see how much of our great tradition we have sustained and, at the same time, to see how boldly we have moved into the future.

C. F. Martin IV

PREFACE

IN THE EARLY SEVENTIES, I found myself teaching art at Blair Academy in Blairstown, New Jersey. If you draw a line from my hometown of Bethlehem, Pennsylvania to Blairstown, it takes you right through the small town of Nazareth. The Martin Guitar Company had erected a billboard on Route 22 advertising their daily factory tours and one day I stopped in. As someone interested in woodworking and music, I was completely amazed by the tour and remember thinking that the factory was probably one of the finest wood shops I had ever encountered.

After the tour I asked the receptionist whether there was any scrap wood. She directed me around to the south side of the building where both dumpsters were overflowing with generous blocks of mahogany and thinner off-cuts of rosewood, ebony, and spruce. I couldn't believe my eyes. I pulled my old Mustang around and filled the back seat and the trunk with wood.

The off-fall was perfect for my woodworking course at Blair. I had never worked with rosewood or mahogany and I returned to the dumpster every few weeks, figuring out that the garbage trucks came on Tuesdays and Fridays, and amassing quite a stack of exotic wood — so much so that I began to be selective in taking only larger or more attractively grained pieces. There was enough mahogany veneer for me to experiment with some simple musical instruments. I built a few mountain dulcimers and bouzouki-like mando-guitars. I stocked the wood shop at Blair and when that was full, I stocked my father's workshop in Bethlehem. Whenever I returned home I always visited Martin to replenish my supplies.

Eventually, I left Blair to take an art teaching job at The Stowe School in Stowe, Vermont and lugged my cache of Martin veneers and woodworking tools off to Vermont. After two years my teaching career screeched to a halt and I returned to Bethlehem, my passion for woodworking in full gear. Regular visits to the Martin dumpster were yielding materials that were ideal for jewelry boxes and stack-laminated turnings. The workers near the dumpster door were starting to recognize me. I was startled one day when one of them came outside while I was picking through the rosewood scraps. His name was Harvey and he was the assistant foreman of the machine room where all the raw wood was cut into parts. He spoke in a very heavy Pennsylvania Dutch accent. "I saved some stuff for ya," said

Harvey, and he handed out a sizeable stack of bookmatched spruce soundboards that had been rejected for small knots and imperfections. I graciously accepted and thanked him.

"What ah ya dew with dis stuff anyhow?"

I had a couple of odd instruments in the car. I reached in and grabbed a mando-guitar with a rosewood top, and a strange drone banjo with a door-knob tuning machine on the headstock designed to produce Ravi Shankar lead runs. Harvey took these inside and paraded them around to the workers. Mr. Martin, who must have been eighty at the time, was walking around the plant and Harvey showed him the "Boak-struments."

"That fellow ought to apply for a job," said C. F.

After several minutes, Harvey brought my instruments back to the dumpster platform and handed them down.

"The old man says you should apply for a job." He pronounced job with a "ch" in front like "chob."

I was definitely not dressed for job hunting. My jeans were torn and slightly soiled with sawdust from the dumpster. My hair was long and unruly. My flannel shirt was faded and I needed a shave, but Harvey's encouraging words prompted me to drive around to the front of the building, brush myself off, and walk in.

"Hello. I'm wondering if there are any job openings?" I smiled.

The receptionist was not amused but replied: "We have one opening but it's very specific. I doubt you'd be qualified."

"What's the position?" I tried to counter her curtness with a firm and confident reply.

"Well, it's a design drafting position. We were actually looking for a college student with some engineering or drafting background." She expected that this would end the conversation.

"I've been teaching drafting for three years. In fact, I have some examples of my ink-on-mylar draftings in the car. That's a specialty of mine." Disappointment was showing on her face. She rose to a new level of defensiveness.

"Well, we're actually looking for someone with some substantial woodworking background." She picked up her emery board and smoothed out a rough edge on her thumbnail.

"Actually, I've been an avid woodworker since I was a boy. I've been teaching woodworking too and I've got some jewelry boxes and lathe turnings in the car. Should I bring them in?"

Below: Stack-laminated bowl from rosewood, mahogany, and maple Martin scraps, with Style-45 abalone banding by Dick Boak, 1977.

She was livid. She gave it one last shot. "You know, it really will be necessary for any applicant to have a working knowledge of musical-instrument making, and a familiarity with the materials we use."

She was playing right into my hands. "I've been making musical instruments and teaching instrument making for several years. I have a few instruments in the car that I made from your scraps. Harvey at the back door told me that Mr. Martin suggested that I apply." I was pushing my luck, but it was worth my strongest push.

"Alright. Bring your things in. I'll see whether Personnel can send someone up front to see you."

Several moments later, I was seated at a table with Ken Murdock, the Assistant Personnel Manager. Excitedly I showed him my draftings, some inlayed jewelry boxes, a few goblets, and three instruments.

"Can you start tomorrow?" he asked.

"No," I replied. "I'm going to see Bob Dylan tomorrow in Philadelphia, but I can begin on Wednesday." His eyes rolled, but he handed me the necessary employment forms. I packed my wares and headed toward the door. As I passed the receptionist, she strained a fake smile.

"I'll see you on Wednesday!" I waved.

Her jaw dropped in disbelief. Her name was Rita. She greeted me upon my arrival two days later, pleased to see that I had better clothes and was capable of bathing. We soon became friends.

That was twenty-seven years ago, as of the writing this book. Since then I have been privileged to spend my weekdays at C. F. Martin & Co. I never mentioned to anyone that I would have gladly worked for free. I have been a draftsman, a maker of prototypes, the manager of the 1833 Shop, the founder of A Woodworker's Dream, the head of the Martin Wood Products division, the coordinator of Darco stringmaking procedure in Mexico, a desktop publisher, the advertising and publicity manager, the head of Artist Relations, and the designer and coordinator of Limited Edition Signature Model guitar projects. More recently, I have facilitated several Martin book projects, this one being the closest to my heart. Some people would say that I have the best job in the world. It's not always as glamorous as it sounds, but it's a wonderful thing to work in a field that is my personal passion. I do very much love my "chob."

"Can you start tomorrow?" he asked. "No," I replied. "I'm going to see Bob Dylan tomorrow in Philadelphia, but I can begin on Wednesday."

Dick Boak

ESTABLISHING A PRECEDENT

FROM THE VERY BEGINNING, C. F. Martin Sr. and the company that was subsequently founded in his name established a precedent of taking unique orders from guitar enthusiasts who desired more than that which was offered as standard. Sometimes this took the form of added ornamentation. Less often it required a physical modification to the shape or design, or the addition of extra strings.

Given the choice, it is likely that each reigning Martin would have preferred to avoid custom work unless business was down or the extra charge was worth the effort. In some cases, the clear benefits from satisfying the whims of a celebrity artist overrode any perceived bother.

Evidence can be found in early production-log entries of guitars with "special ornamentation." Such was the case with Jimmie Rodgers' 1927 request for an ornate 12-fret 000-45 guitar with his name in stylized lettering on the fingerboard. Rodgers' high visibility and popularity no doubt caused many other artists of the day to want their name boldly inlaid to convey their celebrity stature as well. Gene Autry, Tex Fletcher, Roy Rogers, and a host of others followed suit. Sometimes their guitars were customized after the fact by local artisans, but factory customization occurred when policy allowed it.

Perry Bechtel's special requests for a longer neck led to the development of Martin's 14-fret alteration of the traditional 12-fret body. That innovation was certainly one of the more significant breakthroughs in guitar design, making a strong case as to why a company might wish to listen carefully to their customers. Of course for every great idea there will be ninety-nine frivolous ones, but what would American guitars look like today if Martin had disregarded Bechtel's desire to play further up the neck, or ignored Harry Hunt's requests for a large-bodied "Dreadnought" version of the oddly shaped Ditson models?

Much of the innovation in Martin guitar design must be attributed to Frank Henry Martin, who managed the company for the first half of the twentieth century. His son, C. F. Martin III, deserves credit for preserving the integrity of the many designs that evolved under his father's watch. C. F. Martin III (or Mr. Martin as we all called him) was conservative by all accounts. While he was greatly loved and respected, he did restrict one-of-a-kind guitar production, which he considered to be distracting and inefficient.

Mr. Martin's son, Frank Herbert Martin, concurred with that opinion, believing that the company should focus on the popular models like the D-18, the D-28, and perhaps the D-35 — little more. The smaller sizes were tolerated but thought to be a dying breed, and any customization was strongly discouraged. Frank broke policy in 1976 by issuing the Limited Edition D-76 Bicentennial model and the matching Vega V-76 banjo, although with an edition of 1976 guitars, the limited aspect was somewhat questionable.

Chris Martin and I became friends early on in both our careers. We shared a fervent desire to test the waters of Martin guitar design, well outside the traditional or established models offered. Prior to the creation of an official Martin Custom Shop, Chris and I tried our hand at our vision of the perfect guitar. It was a 00-shaped, 12-fret slotted-head guitar with N-20 styled black bindings and the deep body depth of a Dreadnought. For appointments, we chose the torch headstock pattern, an abalone inlaid rosette, scalloped braces, and herringbone top trim. Chris delivered that Custom Shop precursor by hand to a very excited Martin enthusiast in the Midwest.

Spurred on by Chris's conviction that custom guitars could bring significant income, Martin began accepting custom orders in 1979 with Serial #410400 (Custom 01), the first guitar with the "CUSTOM" designation stamped on the front block. I am happy to say that this guitar is my own, since I had the specifications ready to go more than a year in advance of the decision to allow its construction.

By this time, it became very apparent that many of the pre-war Martin models, whose specifications had been subsequently altered or completely discontinued, were very special instruments. Several of our key dealers understood this situation and took advantage of the Custom Shop's capabilities to recreate these highly desirable, vintage-styled instruments.

Noticing the evolving popularity of our Custom Shop, the Nieman Marcus Department Store contacted us with a proposal to make what was, at the time, the most expensive Martin guitar ever created. It was a very fancy D-45 with a "Tree Of Life" inlay on the fingerboard, bridge, pickguard, and headplate. The inlays were beautifully executed by David Nichols of Custom Pearl Inlay who, for many years, cut all the special inlays for the Custom Shop and still does a considerable amount of Martin's custom work. The significance of the Nieman Marcus instrument is that it perhaps initiated what appears to be an unending quest for the most expensive and elaborate Martin guitar — a quest that continues to this day with no signs of dissipation.

David Nichols was a key participant in this quest, as is perhaps best exhibited in an early custom guitar with inlays created by Boston designer Ed Britt. Inspired by the extravagantly engraved

Left: The first official Custom
Shop Martin guitar — Serial
#410400 — made in 1979.
Right: The Nieman Marcus
D-45. Far Right: A Style-7
Martin Mandolin with exquisite
interlocked abalone and
mother-of-pearl inlay.

mother-of-pearl banjo inlays of the first part of the twentieth
century, Ed applied his illustrative and design talents to the many
applicable surfaces of the guitar with remarkable results.

While the Custom Shop was initiated to enable individual
customers — and dealers — to create their own versions of the ideal

What would American guitars look like today if Martin had disregarded Bechtel's desire to play further up the neck, or ignored Harry Hunt's requests for a large-bodied Dreadnought version of the oddly shaped Ditson models?

Martin guitar, an added and unforeseen benefit was that it provided
a vehicle for Martin to produce an unending array of new models and
also to profit in the process. Models that had many recurring
customers could be easily identified and considered for addition to
the line In effect, the Custom Shop had the potential to support
Martin's R&D efforts.

Martin had been dabbling in small editions and, in 1984,
the idea was formalized as the "Guitar Of The Month"
program (GOM). These "GOMs" were either recreations of
vintage Martin models or unique "copied and pasted"
amalgamations of Martin features. The models were
typically prototyped and introduced at the Winter
NAMM (National Association Of Music Merchants)
Show in Anaheim.

With so many original shapes and even more historical
styles, the possibilities for GOM models seemed endless,
and the many models released between 1984 and 1994
represented a tremendous diversity of sizes, styles, and
tonewoods, despite missing the essential ingredient of some
meaningful connection to or acknowledgement of Martin's
rich musical heritage. The "Guitar Of The Month" program
was moderately successful; nevertheless by the mid-nineties the
idea was growing stale, with the design process somewhat erratic
and haphazard.

Far Left: A very ornate Custom 00-45 Delux with inlay pattern by designer Ed Britt, executed by David Nichols of Custom Pearl Inlay. Left: Martin made about ten harp guitars between 1902 and 1912 with varied specifications. This has eighteen strings and a 000 12-fret body. Below: Inspired by the heavy-metal bands of the eighties, Danny Brown in Martin's R&D Department built this double-neck 12-string/6-string model using the oversized Chinery "Goliath" mold.

Martin has had a long-standing policy of not selling guitars directly to the public. This policy evolved as an obvious means of protecting Martin dealers and distributors from being cut out of the picture by direct sales through the factory, so that if famous musicians were to call the factory wanting to buy a guitar — and many did — the policy would be explained and the callers would be promptly redirected to a local Martin dealer.

This scenario occurred often and, while it was certainly good for the dealers, it was detrimental from the standpoint of having any direct feedback or input from working musicians about desirable models and features. In addition, the policy did little to nurture or support Martin's relationships with highly influential artists. The obvious but evasive challenge seemed to be how to initiate and maintain close relationships with artists without interrupting or interfering with dealer sales in the marketplace. The Gene Autry Signature Edition provided a perfect template for future Martin signature models, a well-balanced blend of altruism and art.

In order to facilitate the construction of the prototypes for these and other new model offerings, it became necessary to extract some of Martin's best craftspeople from guitar production and isolate them in an R&D area. Dale Eckhart performed this important job for many years. As the demands on R&D increased, a young and talented Danny Brown brought his unique skills to the department. A fervent fan of Led Zeppelin's Jimmy Page, Danny couldn't contain his enthusiasm when it came to revitalizing and updating Martin's turn-of-the-century harp guitar design. Chris Martin

encouraged Danny and gradually a more modern and practical 6- and 12-string double-neck acoustic was born. Though the model was never offered for sale, it is significant in that a receptiveness to new ideas had clearly emerged.

Eventually Dale Eckhart's talents were badly needed in the area of final assembly. Danny Brown, too, took on the task of managing the sales of guitar kits and parts over at Guitarmaker's Connection, a retail luthier's supply outlet located at the original North Street plant. Tim Teel, a very skilled craftsperson in his own right, had already brought an incredible array of innovation to Martin with his contribution to the X Series, the Concept guitars, and the D-50 project, and in 2001 Tim assumed responsibility for R&D. With a team of skilled coworkers he continues the work that Dale and Danny started, with particular expertise in developing alternative guitar materials and bold new instrument designs.

Under the open-minded leadership of Chris Martin, the company began to grow and change with surprising rapidity. Some traditionalists would criticize Martin for moving forward into new areas, but equal attention was clearly being focused upon the Standard and Vintage Series, the Golden Era® models, and the growing limited-edition offerings. These higher-end models represent some of the finest examples of Martin's guitarmaking expertise in the history of the company. Those who would worry about the preservation of the Martin legacy can allay their concerns. The stories contained in the pages of this book clearly reveal Martin's full commitment to the continuous revitalization of Martin's musical heritage.

PERRY BECHTEL OM-28

A banjo player's request changes the acoustic guitar forever

IN 1993, A PERRY BECHTEL Commemorative OM-28 was conceived to pay tribute to the man who is credited with the development of the 14-fret neck on Martin guitars. Bechtel was well known in the twenties as a master of the plectrum banjo, but as the popularity of the guitar increased, the popularity of tenor and plectrum banjos waned. Bechtel began including the guitar in his repertoire but was frustrated by the lack of access to the upper registers of the neck.

His strong and persistent requests for an extended neck caused Martin to experiment by modifying the 12-fret 000 body shape. The new shape was squarer at the shoulders, with the neck-to-body junction located two half-notes up the fingerboard at the 14th fret. Oddly, 12-fret 000s had long been offered with the longer 25.4-inch scale length. This was carried forward onto the 14-fret version, yielding a very projective and tonally balanced guitar. With a 1¾-inch fingerboard width at the nut and a unique teardrop-shaped pickguard, the new guitar was aptly dubbed the Orchestra Model or "OM." First introduced in 1929, the OMs remained on the pricelist for only four years before being supplanted by the shorter-scale 000 14-fret model that abandoned the teardrop pickguard in favor of a more standard Martin shape.

The Perry Bechtel Commemorative OM-28 became the first Martin Limited Edition to pay tribute to an artist, albeit one that was deceased. Mrs. Perry Bechtel co-signed the interior labels with Chris Martin, and the edition of ninety-four guitars were highly revered by the top fingerstyle guitarists who had long been starved of Martin's vintage OM, a design that is arguably the first and last word in tonality, balance, and player dynamics.

Above: A pair of Brazilian rosewood D-45 Deluxe conversions.
Right: Perry Bechtel, of 14-fret fame, with his plectrum banjo.
Opposite: Top detail of the Perry Bechtel Commemorative OM-28 prototype.

GENE AUTRY
D-45

The re-creation of the first D-45 sets the stage for future collaborations

SHORTLY AFTER THE COMPLETION of the Perry Bechtel edition, Chris visited the impressive Autry Museum Of Western Heritage in the Hollywood Hills. Gene Autry, then well into his eighties, showed Chris his priceless original D-45S, a centerpiece of the museum's collection. Gene had custom-ordered this 12-fret Dreadnought in the early thirties with special ornamentation. Specifically, fancy Style-45 abalone-pearl bordering was stipulated and Gene's name was inlaid in mother-of-pearl script across the fingerboard. This instrument was the very first D-45 ever made and it appeared frequently throughout the movies and recordings of Gene Autry's long and colorful career.

Chris was impressed that Gene had apparently refused in excess of a million dollars from a collector who wanted to purchase the guitar. Upon his return to Nazareth, Chris proposed a collaboration wherein the museum would grant a license to Martin to replicate Gene's D-45. In exchange, Martin would donate a portion of the proceeds from the sale of each instrument to the museum, the royalty thus supporting a nonprofit charity. This altruistic aspect gave the project a particular integrity, in contrast to the often crass merchandising that many other companies applied to their artist endorsements.

There were a number of tricky design challenges to the project

and, as the artist-in-residence of sorts, my help was enlisted in creating the digital artwork that Larry Sifel and Jeff Harding of Pearlworks needed to replicate the fingerboard. My work involved studying old photographs of Gene with the guitar, often in odd perspective, which required trying to skew the proportions so that the lettering could be flattened and accurately re-created.

We weren't exactly sure that consumers would want Gene's name so prominently inlaid, so a second understated version was designed as an option. The prototypes were unveiled at the Anaheim NAMM Show in January of 1994. At the show, dealers placed orders for sixty-six guitars worldwide. With a retail price of $22,000 each, this was perceived as a huge success on all accounts.

Martin's relationship with The Autry Museum Of Western Heritage has remained strong. For two consecutive years during the winter NAMM Show in Los Angeles, we reserved the museum for the annual Martin Dealer Dinner. This gave our customers and sales staff a chance to experience Gene Autry's enduring legacy first hand. Everyone found the exhibits at the museum to be inspirational, lending a perfect atmosphere for evening entertainment with Walden Dahl's cowboy band Coyote, not to mention delicious chuckwagon cuisine in the western tradition.

ERIC CLAPTON 000-42EC

The beginning of an enduring relationship

ON JANUARY 16, 1992 at the Bray Film Studios in Windsor, England, Eric Clapton recorded an extended set of seventeen songs for a television show of increasing popularity: *MTV Unplugged*. The highlights of the show included "Tears From Heaven," an intensely emotional lament that followed the tragic death of Eric's son Conor, plus a slow yet inspired acoustic version of the rock classic "Layla." In fact, every song recorded during that session possessed a fresh magic that seemed to revitalize the nation's appreciation of "unplugged" music, as if this were somehow a newly invented phenomenon.

The subsequent recording went on to win the Grammy Award for Album Of The Year in 1992. By popular demand, MTV re-aired the show incessantly and released a video that yielded unprecedented sales.

It wasn't long before my phone started to ring. Though Eric had used several instruments on the show, the predominant acoustic guitars were Martins and everyone wanted to know exactly what models he was playing.

I did some research and found that two very similar short-scaled 000 14-fret models were used: one was an exquisite 1939 000-42 (Serial #73234) and the other was a 1966 000-28 (Serial #208511) that Martin historian Mike Longworth had converted into a more ornate 000-45. And so the calls came in and I answered the questions, over and over again until, in the wake of the Gene Autry project, it occurred to me that the whole world was ready and waiting for an Eric Clapton Signature Edition.

I sat down with Chris Martin in his office and carefully explained the idea. He responded with enthusiasm and caution in the same

breath, and he encouraged me to proceed in making a proposal to Eric Clapton with one simple caveat: that I follow the basic formula of the Autry project and donate a royalty percentage to charity.

With every ounce of care and empathy that I could muster, I prepared a succinct message for Eric. Enlisting the help of our then publicity agent in the UK, the illustrious Max Kay, I was successful in getting the fax delivered to the office of Eric's manager at that time, Roger Forrester.

A very heartfelt and favorable response came back to us the very next day. We were off and running with tremendous enthusiasm. Eric's longstanding guitar technician Lee Dickson and I began the back-and-forth process of developing the specifications for a special model. It was difficult at the onset since Eric had made a small sketch of an extremely slight cutaway. It was my job to inform him that this was too difficult and costly to implement into production, and the resulting benefits appeared to be minimal at best.

Eric seemed to understand this though, and we proceeded to amalgamate his favorite features of the two 000 Martins. The resulting 000-42EC was prototyped while I carefully reviewed the titles and lyrics of every Clapton recording, looking for a numerical reference that might lend itself to an edition quantity. Inherently I knew that the number needed to be more than one hundred. I also felt that five hundred seemed to be too many. Flipping through his old albums, I landed upon *461 Ocean Boulevard* and everything clicked.

The sales manager thought I was stark raving mad. He sent an inquiry out to the Martin dealers asking them how many $8,200

Left: Sunburst prototype of the groundbreaking 000-42EC Eric Clapton Signature Edition.
Above: The standard non-sunburst 000-42EC with the aged appeal of vintage-toned lacquer.

guitars they would likely order if we were to issue a limited-edition Style-42 guitar. Of course, the Clapton name was not mentioned because we felt it critical to keep the project a complete secret until the introduction date at the Winter NAMM Show. And of course, the dealers responded as expected, with a great deal of skepticism and negativity.

Chris Martin, however, backed me up and we flew out to the show hoping to sell 461 Eric Clapton guitars. They were all gone in a day. Everyone stood there, myself included, scratching their heads in wonder, wishing that Eric could have lived up the street a mile or two, at 1461 Ocean Boulevard. That would have sufficed nicely.

As the 000-42EC models made it through the line, it became clear to us that these instruments were indeed very special: a perfect collaboration with a legendary guitarist and a timeless design to boot. It would be a very tough act to follow.

On route to the international MusikMesse in Frankfurt, Chris Martin, his half-brother Douglas, my wife Susan, and I arranged to meet up with Eric backstage prior to one of his legendary performances at the Albert Hall. There we presented him with guitar number one of the edition plus an oversized mock check for $92,000 made out to The Eric Clapton Charitable Trust. We were treated that evening to Eric's unmatcheable mastery of the guitar.

More than with any other artist, this collaboration became one that evolved naturally to present many further editions, shown in later pages, bringing the Martin 000 deservedly back into the mainstream of modern acoustic music.

Top: Eric Clapton performing with his 1939 vintage 000-42.
Above: Soundboard detail showing the tasteful and elegant Style-42 appointents, an abalone-inlaid snowflake bridge, plus Eric's distinctive signature inlaid in pearl between the 19th and 20th frets.

MARTY STUART
HD-40MS
& TRAVIS TRITT

Hank, horseshoes, and harmonics

ONE AFTERNOON, THE PHONE RANG. It was Marty Stuart, just calling me out of the blue. We had a long conversation about Hank Williams Sr. Marty had been collecting country memorabilia, especially belongings of Hank Williams, and was calling to suggest that Martin consider creating a commemorative guitar that honored Hank.

I liked the idea but was confused about who controlled the estate. There seemed to be a lot of family and nonfamily fingers in the pie and I didn't have a clear idea from Marty who would be the right person or persons with whom to make a proposal, let alone an agreement. Lightheartedly, I suggested to Marty that I'd much rather do a signature-guitar model with him.

"You serious?"

"Sure am," I recoiled.

I'll be damned if he didn't hop on a plane the very next morning. I picked him up at the airport and showed him a great day in Nazareth. I had promised him a lobster tail for lunch to soften the expense of the flight, but he settled for some pasta. After lunch, I took him on a thorough tour of the plant. He was accosted by several hundred autograph seekers as he walked with me through the aisles. Marty was used to all that. He was a real gentleman to everyone, signing sound holes and used squares of sand paper.

Afterwards, we sat down and talked guitars. He had a lot of Martins. One was a D-45 that had apparently belonged to Hank, who in turn had given it to Johnny Cash, who eventually gave it to Marty. There was some controversy about the validity of the story, but Marty seemed to care more about the guitars themselves. An exceptional player himself, he knew exactly what he wanted. It would be based upon a D-28, but scalloped with a vintage quality about it.

The fingerboard inlays were personally designed by Marty, incorporating images of steer horns, horseshoes, dice, hearts, and flowers. He contracted a local inlay artist in Nashville to work up a prototype fingerboard. Upon completion, he sent it to me. I felt that the inlays were slightly out of proportion but still very original, so I made my recommendations to Larry and Jeff at Pearlworks and they modified the artwork in a very tasteful fashion. Ultimately, Pearlworks delivered the final fingerboard design, beautifully executed with more than a hundred pieces of mother-of-pearl, gold pearl, black pearl, abalone shell, and composite stone. Marty's distinctive signature took its position at the final fret in pearl.

One of the more interesting design challenges of the HD-40MS was Marty's concept for a herringbone pearl rosette that was conceived to compliment the

Chris Martin gradually came to call this pattern "The Vine Of Twigs," for the obvious reason that it was practically devoid of leaves.

fine pattern prewar herringbone wood marquetry that he'd specified for the perimeter of the top on his model.

The prototypes were completed just prior the Nashville NAMM Show where they were due to be introduced. Marty was shooting his "Thanks To You" video in a studio warehouse west of town. I drove over with his signature model, and like a kid in a candy shop he dropped everything and became thoroughly immersed with the guitar for half an hour, saying it was one of the best-sounding guitars he'd ever played. That meant a lot to me given that he'd played a ton of Martins, many of which had belonged to the greatest country stars of all time. He used the guitar to record the video that day, and he stayed in touch during the following months that the edition guitars went into production.

The edition was limited to 250 guitars. We considered this number ambitious, but they all sold out very quickly, certainly a testament to the respect that people have for Marty's musicianship. Bob Dylan's management called one day wanting information about the model. Bob had seen and played one that he loved, but it belonged to someone else. I tried to track a few models down for Dylan, but nothing ever materialized. Some time later Marty Stuart and Travis Tritt were traveling together during their Double Trouble tour. Marty's model had certainly caught Travis's attention and one afternoon they descended upon the factory under separate cover, Marty in a Checker cab and Travis in a gigantic black limo. The production of Marty's model was in full swing and I took them on a special tour.

Afterwards, we all sat down and Travis rattled off specifications for what was at the time the most expensive Brazilian rosewood custom Martin guitar ever constructed. He wasn't sure, however, exactly what he wanted on the finger-board. I happened to have my Custom OM 12-String Deluxe Cutaway with my "Vine Of Harmonics" inlay pattern. I had drawn this pattern based upon fractional subdivisions of the scale length. The tiny spines terminating each branch were intended to have some significance to the astute slide player. Not only did my design have little practicality but Chris Martin gradually came to call this pattern "The Vine Of Twigs," for the obvious reason that it was practically devoid of leaves. As a last-ditch effort to salvage my concept, I added the tiny wishbone that was a subtle reference to my most prized possession — the incredibly fragile wishbone of a hummingbird that I had found in the grass as a child.

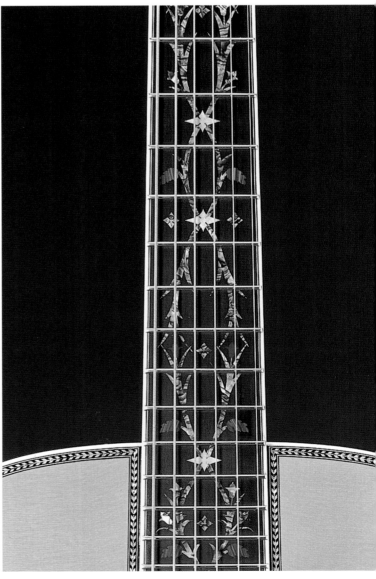

Travis found some solace in this odd pattern and chose it for his guitar, but he had the sense to request that the inlay artists at Pearlworks take poetic license in choosing a wider variety of colors from their pallet of shell and composite stone.

Travis's guitar was magnificent; twigs, wishbones and all, and we are most honored to see him show up occasionally on a TV special or video cradling it in his arms. I think Travis took particular pride in the fact that he had out-performed Marty in the ornamentation department. He called to say:

"Hello Dick! This is Travis Tritt calling — I just want to let you know I got the guitar. It is absolutely fabulous. It is a beautiful instrument. I'm thrilled with it and thanks again. Beautiful, beautiful piece of work and I'm gonna really enjoy playing it."

Marty was thrilled too, but for a different reason. He was the first country musician to be honored with an edition and his enthusiasm didn't end there. My conversations with Marty often strayed to brainstorming about other potential bluegrass and deserving country guitar players. Marty had been married to Johnny Cash's daughter Cindy and though they were long since divorced, Marty had maintained a very strong tie with Johnny. We both thought a Johnny Cash model would be a winner, so Marty made the call for me. In a matter of days, I received a very enthusiastic handwritten fax from Johnny and we were on our way.

Left: Travis Tritt's Custom D-45. Top: Detail of Marty Stuart's HD-40MS fingerboard. Bottom: Detail of Travis's "Vine of Harmonics" fingerboard.

IT SEEMED PRETTY OBVIOUS that the "Man in Black" would want a black guitar. In fact, in addition to the wide assortment of Martins in his collection, Johnny already owned a black D-35 that he used as his primary stage guitar.

After receiving his encouraging letter, we went back and forth a few times with some ideas. With assistance from Johnny's guitar technician Brian Farmer we arrived at specifications for an elegant D-42 model with thirteen pearl-bordered abalone stars as position markers and Johnny's signature at the last fret. The completion of the prototypes coincided nicely with the Telluride Bluegrass Festival. Since I had planned to attend Telluride and since Johnny was due to perform, I took the prototype across the country and up that beautiful mountain, eventually meeting up with Johnny and his wife June Carter Cash backstage behind their tour bus.

Johnny looked weary, but he and June were gracious and warm. He loved the guitar. It's hard to not get excited over such a piece of personalized art. We took the opportunity to get some informal photos of Johnny with the guitar. In the middle of all of this, up comes Stormin' Norman Schwartzkopf, a longtime friend of Johnny's. As they both explained, they often meet up on tour. Norman likes to sing and play some guitar too.

I found the General refreshing and easy going. We talked while Johnny strummed. This was eventually broken up by the urgency of the performance. He did well that night, considering that his illness would get much worse in the months that followed.

Despite the high retail price of the model the edition still sold eighty pieces. After the fact, we figured that many of Johnny's fans didn't have a lot of money anyway, but the people who own those guitars sure love them... especially Johnny Cash himself. His heart was broken when he fell with the number-one guitar onstage and it was damaged rather badly. It came limping back to Nazareth in its UPS carton. The people in the Repair Department brought it back to life just around the time that Johnny started recovering from his illness.

The Johnny Cash Signature Model guitars were stunning. While recording a television special together, Johnny's close friend Willie Nelson saw and performed with Johnny's D-42JC signature model. With Willie's interest fully sparked, Marty Stuart once again rose to the challenge and furnished me with a mysterious phone number with a Texas area code. I dialed it.

Left: Johnny Cash at Telluride with the D-42JC prototype. Above: Three views of Johnny's black-lacquered D-42JC showing the abalone-inlaid soundhole and signature detail, the three-piece back, and the Style-45 bound headstock.

WILLIE NELSON
N-20WN & N-20WNB
The legendary "Trigger" pulls into town

THE PHONE TONES PULSED, THEN…

"Hello."

"Yes, ah, hello. I'm trying to get in touch with Willie Nelson?"

"This is Willie," said Willie. Marty had given me the cell phone on Willie's bus. I was a bit startled to be talking to Willie so directly.

Willie was smooth as silk. He was very interested in having his old Martin guitar Trigger replicated, undeniably one of the most famous and recognizable instruments on the planet. In the late sixties, Willie had had an inexpensive "Conn" nylon stringed guitar with an ingenious onboard pickup. One night, it got badly damaged during a show and Willie took it in to Shot Jackson's in Nashville to be repaired. Shot couldn't fix it, but he had a brand new Martin N-20 hanging on the wall.

"Can you put the pickup from that thing into the Martin?" asked Willie.

"Sure can," said Shot.

It's a gas to look at photos of Willie and that guitar through the years. Willie was clean cut when the guitar was new. A decade later, his hair was shoulder length and the N-20 had a few scratches and dents. By the mid-eighties, the guitar was starting to show some serious wear and so was Willie, but he didn't want to get it fixed. The sound was just right, in spite of the fact that there was a sizeable hole worn right through the soundboard. The guitar had become such an integral part of Willie's sound that he invited his closest friends and band members to sign the guitar and soon it was covered with legendary names: Johnny Cash, Kris Kristofferson, Merle Haggard, and a hundred more.

So when the IRS got on Willie's case, it's no surprise that the first thing he did was hide that guitar away. It sat safely in his manager's office for months until things cooled down a bit.

Willie was scheduled to do a concert in Valley Forge just outside Philadelphia. I made plans to meet him there so that I could talk measurements and take some photos of Trigger. After the show, I waited backstage with Waylon Jennings and a hundred middle-aged women. Finally "Poodie," Willie's stage manager, came to get me and Waylon. Those women were just about in tears with envy. I hopped up on the bus and there he was, smooth as silk, relaxing at his table. He stood up to greet us.

Willie was a complete gentleman. He handed Trigger to me and I gave it a thorough inspection and a strum, taking measurements and noting my observations into a sketchbook. After twenty-five minutes or so, Willie decided he was ready to go outside and sign autographs for the several hundred fans that were waiting. I realized then that I, too, needed his autograph in order to create the digital artwork for the pearl inlaid signature on the fingerboard. I handed Willie my notebook opened up to a blank page. He reached out with his Sharpie and made a squiggle. I looked at it in disbelief. It was completely illegible.

I didn't want to insult Willie, but I handed the notebook back to him and said: "Willie, I need you to do it again; this time a little more recognizable."

Above: Willie's "horse," the original Martin N-20, personally dubbed "Trigger."

He squiggled again, albeit this time a slightly more intelligible squiggle, but a squiggle just the same. I sighed and accepted this as the reality of the situation.

Returning to Nazareth inspired to initiate the prototypes, I created a small silhouette of the state of Texas with a lone star in the center. The word "Trigger" seemed an appropriate marker for the octave fret. My friends at Fishman created a beautiful and very limited version of Willie's pickup. Everything came together nicely. When the prototypes were complete, I called to check Willie's schedule and was amazed to find that he was going to play the State Theater in Easton, just ten miles from Nazareth, in a number of weeks. I made arrangements to meet him the afternoon of the show in the parking lot of the Larry Holmes Commodore Inn across the river into Jersey. I arrived at two and Willie's security chief Larry Gorman informed me that Willie was still asleep. At three, I was summoned. I grabbed the prototype and climbed up the steps onto Willie's bus.

This time it was just Willie and me. He looked at the prototype with great interest and compared it to the genuine Trigger. We joked about creating a "Willie Machine" that could play the guitar real hard in just the right spots so as to replicate a worn hole through the top.

Before we knew it, it was time to depart for soundcheck. Willie suggested that I leave my car and drive over on the bus. We crossed the toll bridge and exited onto 4th Street.

The Easton Circle was under major construction. There was a tiny sign at the end of the exit ramp that said: "No Busses or Trucks In Construction Area." Of course, that sign was a few feet off the ground so that cars could read it clearly, but in the tour bus, we were twelve feet off the ground. The driver proceeded boldly toward the circle.

Two lanes became one and the bus came to a halt. It was impossible to turn at the circle. There simply wasn't enough clearance. The driver tried to back up, but there were several dozen cars behind us waiting to get through. The stalemate lasted long enough to attract a young police officer. He banged his fist on the bus door. Willie said: "Just relax everybody. This bus has diplomatic immunity. We're a separate country."

Our driver (all six and a half feet of him) slipped off the bus and closed the door. There was a good bit of verbal wrangling and finally, the frustrated officer settled on issuing a $350 traffic violation. He had no idea who Willie Nelson was, not that that would have made any difference. He cleared the cars in back of us and supervised the slow de-vacuation of the bus. Soundcheck would just have to wait.

After the show, Willie was greeting people on stage. He had both versions of Trigger and several people snapped some photos. The guitars raised some nice royalties for Farm Aid, the mayor of Easton intervened to void Willie's ticket, and life returned to some sense of normalcy for everyone, except of course Willie.

Above: Willie and "Trigger" at Farm Aid 2002. Right: "Trigger" reincarnated as the N-20WN.

JIMMIE RODGERS
000-45JR

"The Singing Brakeman" — America's first folk singer

I HAD BECOME FASCINATED with Martin 000 12-fret models. These were the largest of the tight-waisted 12-frets. In my opinion, the 000 12-fret guitars seemed to be the most tonally responsive models that Martin had ever made. They were very well balanced, deep, rich, loud, and visually quite beautiful. The long scale and the slotted head contributed to a sweetness and neck resonance simply not present on other Martin models.

The tracing patterns for all the Martin models were kept in metal drawers out where the tops were rosetted and braced. I often referred to these patterns. The 000 12-fret pattern was stamped "Merle Haggard." The word was that Merle had specially ordered a batch of six guitars, one of which had Merle's name inlaid in large block letters.

My good friend and fellow Martin enthusiast from Japan, Juta Sugai, had placed a Custom Shop order for his dream instrument, a 12-fret 000-45. After I saw his guitar come to fruition, I desperately wanted one too. Juta's only disappointment with the guitar was that Martin had replaced the slotted square tapered headstock shaping fixture with a modern version that was neither square nor tapered. To him, it just didn't look right. I agreed. I pleaded with the Custom Shop and Martin production supervisors to reinstate the old headstock dimensions, but this was simply not a priority at the time.

Eventually, the 000 12-fret topic came up in a conversation with Eric Schoenberg and luthier T. J. Thompson, who had an unusual collaborative arrangement with Martin to produce Soloist model guitars under the Schoenberg brand. When I explained my headstock dilemma, Eric and T. J. offered to fabricate a special vintage-styled neck and run it through Martin Custom Shop as a Schoenberg. I agreed, especially given that with this arrangement, I was allowed to furnish an unusual set of Brazilian rosewood that I had been saving for a special project.

That Schoenberg/Martin Custom 12-fret 000-42, with its bar frets and period bracing, was executed in a style that certainly would have made Martin craftsmen of the twenties proud. I showed the guitar to my coworkers. Many already recognized the value and marketability of reviving features from the past, but this guitar provided a workable template for a slightly simpler but still exquisite 000-28GE Golden Era® model, introduced in January of 1996.

Lester Wagner worked at Martin for forty-seven years. At the time of his retirement in 1991, he held the record for the most years of service (except of course for C. F. Martin III!). It would be hard to find a person who loved Martin guitars or knew about them as much as Lester did. He often returned to the factory to visit his friends in Customer Service. In February of 1996, on the heels of the very successful introduction of the 000-28GE Golden Era® model, Lester popped into my office to inform me that the 100th anniversary of Jimmie Rodgers' birthday was forthcoming. He felt that a Jimmie Rodgers commemorative guitar might be in order, especially since any potential production kinks would be resolved with the engineering of the 000-28GE. I thought it was a great idea. I didn't know a very much about Jimmie Rodgers but I was about to learn.

Jimmie was America's first folk singer. He is widely acknowledged to be the "Father Of Country Music" and affectionately referred to as "America's Blue Yodeler." During his railroad days his fans called him "The Singing Brakeman."

Jimmie Rodgers' original 1927 12-fret 000-45 with special "Blue Yodel" ornamentation on the headstock and "Jimmie Rodgers" letters inlaid in pearl in the fingerboard.

Born James Charles Rodgers on September 8, 1897, in Meridian, in his early years he traveled the country extensively with the railroad, where he was exposed to many indigenous styles of music. He began to combine these diverse influences in his own songs and in 1927, at the age of thirty, he auditioned for an RCA Victor talent scout. The rest, as they say, is history.

Immediately after being signed, Jimmie Rodger's placed an order for a very special Martin 000-45 guitar. With its Adirondack red-spruce soundboard, forward-shifted scalloped X-bracing, Brazilian rosewood back and sides, and top-of-the-line Style-45 appointments, the guitar was fancy enough, but he still requested additional special ornamentation. The order specified that the headstock be inlaid with Jimmie's trademark "BLUE YODELER" in Martin Style-45 letters. Martin had difficulty fitting all of the "YODELER" letters on the narrow strip between the two peghead slots. As a result, it was agreed to shorten the inlay design to read simply "BLUE YODEL." He also requested that his full name be inlaid into the fingerboard in stylized mother-of-pearl letters. The ebony bridge was ordered with Maltese snowflakes cut from abalone.

Another very unique aspect of the guitar is the hand painted "THANKS" in large letters on the back. After each show, Jimmie would flip the guitar over to the delight of the crowd.

It is certain that C. F. Martin III (1896–1986) personally presented the original 000-45 Blue Yodel guitar to Jimmie, though there is some confusion as to where the presentation occurred. A paragraph on the door of the safe in the Jimmie Rodgers Museum, where the guitar is secured and displayed, states: "Presented to Jimmie Rodgers in Washington, D.C. by Mr. C. Frederick Martin, President of The Martin Guitar Co., July 27, 1927." A letter in the archives, however, suggests that the guitar was presented in New York. Others seem to think it happened in Camden or Trenton, NJ. The guitar itself bears an interior label in C. F. Martin III's own handwriting that reads: "To Jimmie Rodgers, America's Blue Yodeler, with all good wishes. C. Frederick Martin, July 27, 1927."

In any event, Mr. Martin did present the instrument in person. Museum lore has it that Jimmie received sixteen curtain calls on *Frankie & Johnnie* after his performance with his new guitar that night. He stole the show.

At his peak, the recordings of Jimmie Rodgers had the greatest worldwide sales of any other recording artist to date. His music influenced several successive generations of folk, blues, and country stars. His career lasted only a short five years. He died while recording his last record in New York City on May 26, 1933, at the age of thirty-five, a victim of tuberculosis.

His casket was returned by railroad to his birthplace in Mississippi. Many thousands of people are said to have lined both sides of the tracks at every town along the train route. He undoubtedly had a very significant impact on the heart and culture of our nation.

After his passing, the special guitar was returned to his widow, Carrie Rodgers. One evening, she heard Ernest Tubb playing familiar Jimmie Rodgers songs on the radio. She was quite moved by this and eventually attended one of Ernest's shows in person. After the show she introduced herself and their friendship ensued. She eventually loaned Jimmie's 000-45 to him and he used the guitar for more than forty years.

A pickguard was not standard on this model and it is believed that Ernest Tubb added the one to cover the severe playing wear that Jimmie inflicted upon the guitar.

Ernest performed all over the country with Jimmie's 000-45. He was playing in a small club one night and had set the guitar down on the edge of the stage. He picked up another guitar, sang a song, then reached down for his 45. It was gone. Stolen! Ernest told the audience right away that his prized guitar was missing. They formed a huge hand-held circle around the room and the whole place was scoured, looking for the guitar. It wasn't there. Members of the audience volunteered to go around the neighborhood looking for it, checking the small clubs and bars. About five blocks away, in a small dingy club, they found the guitar leaning up against a barstool. The drunk who had walked off with it had no idea what he had. Ernest was so happy to get the instrument back that he didn't even press charges. Nor did he ever tour with the guitar again. He didn't ever want to risk losing it.

After Ernest died, the 000-45 guitar was returned to Jimmie Rodgers' daughter Anita Rodgers Court, since Carrie had passed away. Anita made arrangements to donate the guitar to the Smithsonian Institution, but declined when she learned that they wouldn't display the guitar on a permanent basis.

Above: Soundhole and pyramid bridge detail of the 1996 12-fret 000-28GE Golden Era® edition. Right: Ernest Tubb displaying the flip side of the Jimmie Rodgers 000-45.

ERNEST TUBB RECORD SHOPS

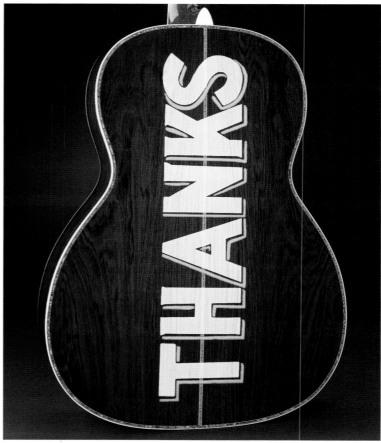

Elsie McWilliams, Jimmie Rodgers' sister-in-law, co-authored many of Jimmie's songs, and her daughter, Pat Ward, eventually convinced Anita to donate the guitar to the Jimmie Rodgers Museum in Meridian, Mississippi. Pat wrapped it up in an old quilt, put it on the back seat of the car and drove it all the way from San Antonio, Texas to Meridian, Mississippi without stopping. That's where the guitar has been ever since.

The original Jimmie Rodgers 000-45 is one of the most valuable (if not priceless) Martin guitars ever made. The museum stores it in a vault and insures it for more than a million dollars. It was Jimmie's personal and favorite guitar. and he made nearly all of his popular recordings with it. In addition to the guitar's colorful history, 000-45 models from that era are very rare and sought-after on the vintage market.

In May of 1996, Martin prototype maker Dale Eckhart and I flew down to the small city of Meridian, Mississippi to visit the Jimmie Rodgers Museum and meet Bob Luke, at that time President of the Board Of Directors of The Jimmie Rodgers Foundation. The archives and vault were opened for us and with Derek Berron's help we took extensive photographs and measurements of the legendary, original guitar.

Dale and I returned to Nazareth very excited about the project. I began the arduous task of scanning the photographs and isolating all the inlays into true-to-scale digital format so that they could be precisely reproduced. I was also able to recreate accurate color separations of the painted "THANKS" lettering from which a decal replica, optional upon request, was made. In the meantime, Dale was selecting parts and beginning the construction of two prototypes. As we progressed, I began writing the text to promote the guitar in Issue #2 of the Martin newsletter, "The Sounding Board."

Then one afternoon an alarming fax came in from a legal group that represented Jimmie Dale Court, son of Anita Rodgers Court and grandson of Jimmie Rodgers. Jimmie Dale lived in Austin, Texas and was aware of our project. As an heir to the estate he was receiving regular payments from the Foundation which our royalties were indirectly supporting. Nonetheless, the fax warned that if Martin were to proceed with the introduction of a Jimmie Rodgers model, a lawsuit would surely be filed on behalf of the client.

I was shattered, but I worked relentlessly with Martin's legal council and Bob Luke to negotiate with Jimmie Dale Court's lawyers. It was a slow and frustrating process and it seemed possible that all our hard work might go down the drain. My hair turned noticeably from brown to gray during those months. With the prototypes complete and on the shelf, I deleted the Jimmie Rodgers text from "The Sounding Board" and resigned myself to the cancellation of the project.

Then the phone rang. Jimmie Dale Court had been found dead in a Texas hotel room, an apparent drug overdose. How were we to react to that news?

When the dust settled, we received great encouragement and help from Ruth Roe, the executor of the Rodgers estate. As a second agreement was drafted, the plot took a strange turn. Jimmie Dale

> ## Pat wrapped it up in an old quilt, put it on the back seat of the car and drove it all the way from San Antonio, Texas to Meridian, Mississippi without stopping.

Court's lawyers also represented the estates of several other legendary figures. Without their client, these attorneys became receptive to a settlement that indemnified Martin and paved the way for a future Hank Williams Sr. commemorative edition, which proved in a rather tragic fashion that even dark clouds can have silver linings.

The prototype was rushed to its introduction at the California NAMM Show in January of 1996 and a special supplement to "The Sounding Board" was quickly published. I was very gratified to be able to present guitar number one of the edition to Ruth Roe and the folks from the Jimmie Rodgers Museum in May, 1996 at the annual Jimmie Rodgers Festival. Marty Stuart assisted with the emotional presentation and christened it with an appropriate and superb rendition of Jimmie's famous song "T For Texas."

Upper Left: Soundhole and bridge detail of the edition guitar, complete with C. F. Martin III's personalized label. Upper Right: Jimmie Rodgers commissioned a sign painter to add the word "THANKS" to his guitar, a feature replicated in decal form for the edition.

HANK SNOW
D-45
Mike Longworth's ultimate snow-job

HANK SNOW — "THE SINGING RANGER" — passed away at the age of eighty-five on December 20, 1999 at his "Rainbow Ranch" home north of Nashville. A veteran inductee in the Country Music Hall Of Fame, he was one of Canada's greatest country stars and perhaps the last surviving link to the rhinestone-encrusted glory days of the Grand Ol' Opry.

Three weeks after his passing, Marty Stuart called to let us know that he would be sending Hank's famous Martin guitar to Nazareth for some careful refurbishment. The instrument (Serial #209319) was a 1966 Brazilian rosewood D-28 that had been converted into a D-45 by Martin's longstanding historian and pearl-inlay artist Mike Longworth. The old guitar hadn't been played a lot in the later years of Hank's life and was in need of a neck reset, some fret work, and some general maintenance.

Marty always knew the right thing to do. I think he wanted to do justice to the memory of Hank Snow by helping to preserve the special guitar. It was also a meaningful show of support for Hank's widow Minnie Snow and for his son Jimmie Rodgers Snow.

A "Hank Snow" fingerboard, also inlaid by Mike Longworth, had been on display in the Martin Museum for nearly two decades. Mike had explained to me that the fingerboard was an extra of sorts, discarded because it wasn't quite what Hank wanted. I was very familiar with that fingerboard, but I had never seen Hank's actual guitar.

When the guitar arrived by courier, the box was very cold to the touch. I carefully unpacked it and let it acclimatize to room temperature and when I finally opened the case, I was spellbound. The guitar was extremely lavish, if not slightly eccentric in its abundance of ornamentation. The incredible leather case was possibly even more ornate than the guitar. It had been custom hand-tooled on every available surface with amazing detail. The guitar and its case were so special that prior to initiating the repair work, I requested permission from the family to take some professional photographs for the Martin archives. Though it didn't seem appropriate so soon after his passing, it certainly occurred to me that somewhere down the line, the guitar would be a great and deserving candidate for a Hank Snow Commemorative Edition.

Gentleman that he always has been, Marty Stuart offered to pick up half the cost of the refurbishment. Martin picked up the other half

as a gesture of good will. When the instrument was finished, we shipped it back to Minnie and Jimmie in Tennessee. I'm sure they were thankful to Marty and to Martin. When someone like Hank Snow dies, their possessions take on a different meaning. That is certainly true of the guitar: the songs that echoed through its wood, the scores of musicians who held, played, and marveled at it, the sweat and toil that Mike Longworth imparted to it during its conversion, and the obvious value that Hank placed upon it — most simply, the guitar is an enduring symbol, if not an embodiment of Hank Snow's well-traveled life.

Above: Hank Snow's famous D-28, converted by Mike Longworth in the D-45 Style.
Below: Hank's custom hand-tooled leather case rivaled the lavishness of his guitar.

MERLE HAGGARD 000C-28SMH

The triumphant return of The Blue Yodel

MERLE HAGGARD IS SYNONYMOUS with great country music. In a career spanning five decades, he has chronicled a world of hard knocks, pain, love, and triumph in songs that show a storyteller's soul. After thirty-nine chart-topping country hits and more than seventy albums, he continues to build on a legacy virtually unmatched in music, country or otherwise. He's also had quite a history with Martin guitars, most likely attributed to his extreme reverence for the "The Father Of Country Music," Jimmie Rodgers.

The music of Jimmie Rodgers had an immense impact on a young Merle Haggard and so did the 12-fret 000-45 that Jimmie played (see page 28). Merle was so enthralled with the instrument that in the sixties he made arrangements with Shot Jackson in Nashville to have Martin make seven special 12-fret 000s. Shot received one of the guitars for doing the deal and gradually Merle sold the others off, but he kept the most special one for himself. He's pictured on the cover of his Jimmie Rodgers tribute album, *Same Train, Different Time* with

I wasn't surprised but I was thrilled when Joe McNamara, our District Sales Manager in Northern California, called to say that Merle was interested in acquiring one of the Jimmie Rodgers 000-45 Commemorative Edition guitars. While waiting for the guitar to be built, however, Merle experienced some serious health problems that caused him to cancel the order.

The silver lining was of course that in the process we did get to know Merle pretty well and during a tour of the East Coast in the spring of 2000, Merle's tour bus pulled in to the Martin parking lot at 7:30 in the morning. We all went out to breakfast at the Nazareth Diner and over scrambled eggs, crisp bacon, and a few helpings of scrapple, we hashed out the basics of the Merle Haggard Signature Edition. Of course, Merle's special bond with Jimmie Rodgers was acknowledged in the 000 12-fret size and by the slotted headstock that referenced Merle's Jimmie Rodgers tribute "Blue Yodel No. 13." The guitar takes a radical departure from tradition with its unique Venetian cutaway — the first time a Martin 12-fret model was ever offered with a cutaway.

The Merle Haggard signature guitar is the first Martin 12-fret model ever offered with a cutaway.

the same guitar. During the late seventies, Merle was playing in Reno, Nevada with the late great Roger Miller. It wasn't a good time for Merle. He had had a bad show and in a moment of angst, he smashed the guitar. Merle relayed to me how sick he has felt about that incident ever since. He had the guitar fixed up but it was never quite the same.

Out in the middle of Martin production, there is a filing cabinet where all the brace tracing patterns are kept. In my early days as draftsman, I was referencing these patterns to create top assembly drawings when I came upon a 12-fret 000 template stamped "Merle Haggard Model." Not knowing the whole story, I was very curious, especially since for my personal taste, the 000 12-fret models exemplify the very best Martin guitars can offer.

Merle Haggard's signature was inlaid in mother-of pearl at the final fret and the interior label was co-signed with Chris Martin. Merle stipulated that the charitable proceeds from the sale of each guitar be donated in support of the Mandan, Arikara, and Hidatsa Native American Tribes Of North Dakota. An edition of 122 special guitars was offered, all selling out quickly, aided by the fact that Merle made a special effort to attend the model unveiling at the Anaheim NAMM Show in January of 2001. There he quickly assembled a great little band that performed to a delighted crowd at the Martin booth. We also took the opportunity to present Merle with an appropriate memento — a rosewood guitar back, complete with the famous "THANKS" decal and a special engraved plaque from one of the Jimmie Rodgers 000-45JR Commemorative Edition guitars.

Unprecedented access to the upper registers of the 12-fret 000 was achieved with Merle Haggard's signature model, enhanced with the elegant combination of herringbone trim with an abalone rosette. Note Merle's understated signature in pearl at the final fret.

HANK WILLIAMS

D-28HW

A *tribute* to the Opry's *lonesome lyricist*

MARTY STUART, A LONGTIME FAN and collector of Hank Williams Sr. memorabilia, had recommended that we honor the country legend in the first place and following a convoluted series of events, we had arrived at a point where the lawyers and agents at CMG had put an agreement together that provided for royalties to the estate. Hank Williams Jr. and his half-sister Jett Williams were the heirs. Appropriately, both are musicians, as is Hank Jr.'s son Hank III.

Hank Jr. had always been a Martin enthusiast, though his style of music carried him into the realm of electric guitars. To help preserve his father's legacy, he set up the Hank Williams Jr. Family Tradition Museum in Nashville. We established communications quickly with Hank Jr. in order to glean whatever information we could about the original Martin guitars that Hank Sr. had owned. Marty Stuart was already in possession of a D-45 that had apparently belonged to him, but the D-28 was perhaps the Martin model most associated with Hank Sr., especially in vintage photographs from that era. Neil Young also owns a D-28 that belonged to Hank, but there was a more significant one on display at the Family Tradition Museum that was passed along through the family after Hank Sr.'s death. That is the instrument we focused our attention on.

The original Hank Williams D-28 Martin (Serial #87422 made in 1944) is one of the most valuable (if not priceless) guitars ever made. Its worth is certainly affected by the fact that it was Hank's favorite personal guitar. He made nearly all his popular recordings with his Martin and he performed with it extensively.

The son of a railroad engineer, Hank Williams was born in Alabama in 1923. Unable to read or write music, he first learned to play with the help of an Alabama street singer named Rufe Payne. Williams launched his career as leader of a small group, the Drifting Cowboys, who performed on local radio shows in Shreveport, Louisiana, and Montgomery, Alabama. By 1949, he had become a nationally acclaimed star of the Grand Ole Opry. A superb songwriter, Williams is remembered for his unique ability to reach people's souls with honest and simple lyrics and music. Among his best-known songs are the classics "Take These Chains From My Heart," "I'm So Lonesome I Could Cry," "Your Cheatin' Heart," "You Win Again," and "I Can't Help It." He died in 1953 and has subsequently been inducted into both the Country Music and Rock And Roll Halls Of Fame. Although Hank Williams Sr., died before reaching the age of thirty, he created a body of work that has made him a legend and earned him a lasting international reputation.

The 75th anniversary of his birth was celebrated in 1998. He was certainly one of the most popular and influential figures in the history of American music and it seemed especially fitting that the D-28HW Hank Williams Signature Edition was introduced concurrent with that anniversary. Constructed with Brazilian rosewood back and sides and inlaid with Hank Williams Sr.'s signature in pearl at the last fret, the commemorative edition utilized prewar Golden Era® features to closely recreate the original guitar. Only 150 instruments were offered for sale and they all sold out shortly after their introduction.

Appropriately, Hank Williams Jr., his (and his father's) legendary manager and songwriter Senator Merle Kilgore, Jett Williams, and her equally legendary attorney and manager and eventual husband Keith Adkinson, were the first four people to take delivery of the Hank Williams Sr. 75th Anniversary guitars.

Left: The Hank Williams Sr. D-28HW Commemorative Edition closely follows the simple appointments and tonal power of Martin's pre-WWII Brazilian rosewood Dreadnought design

Above: Hank Williams Sr. steps up to
the microphone with his 1944 D-28.

The original Hank Williams D-28 Martin is one of the most
valuable guitars ever made. Its worth is certainly affected by
the fact that it was Hank's favorite personal guitar.

KITTY WELLS HTA
The reincarnation of the Honky Tonk Angel

LIKE ANY OTHER HEALTHY AMERICAN male, Chris Martin was clicking through his channel changer one evening when he landed upon a documentary tribute to Kitty Wells on one of the country stations. There she was with her Martin Dreadnought, singing her heart out. Not having had any major exposure to Kitty Wells, Chris came away enamored with her story. The next morning, he pulled the Country Music Foundation Archives book simply titled *Country Music* off the shelf and looked Kitty up in the index. There she was again — a modest and lovely vision in a white dress, smiling with her D-28.

Chris showed the book to me and my Artist Relations associate Chris Thomas, suggesting that we try to find contact numbers for Kitty's management so that we could propose a signature edition in honor of her incredible contribution to American music. It didn't take long before we were in touch with Kitty's manager Norm Blanchard and her grandson John Sturdivant, Jr. of Junction Records in Nashville. Norm, John, and Kitty were all excited by our proposal and we started a discussion about the various Martin guitars that she had owned throughout her long career. There were many, but one stood out in Kitty's memory. The guitar had been stolen many years ago, and although she didn't remember all of its unique aspects, Kitty thought the Country Music Hall Of Fame might be able to furnish a photo of that Custom Dreadnought. She loved the warmth and power of the D-size, but she also loved the comfort of the smaller-bodied Martins. In 2001, we had successfully produced the Beck model that addressed this issue by combining the D shape with the thinner 000 depth. Kitty, too, was intrigued with this idea, and so the thinbody Dreadnought provided the basis for the Kitty's signature edition.

At Kitty's prompting, Chris Thomas had searched for and found some great silhouettes of angels. After all, it was Kitty's hit "It Wasn't God Who Made Honky Tonk Angels" that caused a country music revolution in 1952. The song became the first in the genre by a woman to sell a million copies and reach Number One on country charts. It opened the doors wide for women in country, and launched the careers of Kitty Wells and Johnny Wright, her partner in music and in life.

The best of the angels was a delicate art-nouveau silhouette with outstretched wings. I tried to give this poor angel a country flair with the inclusion of lassos, ten-gallon hats, and halos, but these attempts just cheapened the original image. We scaled the image to the proportion of the headstock. It looked so good up there all by itself against a background of polished black ebony, even the Martin logo seemed unnecessary. An abalone and pearl crown inlaid at the 5th fret acknowledged Kitty's rightful title as the "Queen of Country Music."

The HTA "Honky Tonk Angel" Signature Edition combined an Engelmann spruce soundboard with East Indian rosewood back and sides to achieve an impressive tonal responsiveness. Vintage features such as fine pattern herringbone, grained ivoroid binding, and beveled and polished tortoise-colored pickguard gave the model an integrity worthy of such a legend.

Each Martin HTA Honky Tonk Angel Signature Edition bears an interior label signed by Kitty Wells, Johnny Wright, and Chris Martin. The charitable proceeds from the sale of each guitar were donated in support of MusiCares, which was established by the Recording Academy in 1989. The mission of MusiCares is to ensure that music people have a place to turn in times of need, focusing the resources of the music industry on human-service issues which directly impact the health and welfare of the music community.

The prototype of the edition was presented to Kitty on the stage of the Ryman Auditorium during a special tribute for Kitty and Johnny. When the model was actually unveiled at the Summer NAMM Show in July of 2002, Kitty and Johnny held court in the Martin booth for several hours — signing autographs and posing for photographs with fans.

Seventy beautiful guitars were made and, like the Honky Tonk Angel on the headstock of each guitar, they're strung tight like a spring, waiting to respond to a gentle touch.

Above: Johnny Wright and Kitty Wells with Jack Anglin (right), circa 1950. Left: Kitty's HTA Honky Tonk Angel Signature Edition guitar.

GEORGE JONES D-41GJ

Pearl and scallops for The Possum

ONE AFTERNOON WE RECEIVED A CALL from MCA Records in Nashville. They were fishing for a D-45V as a birthday gift for George Jones. After we relayed the basic cost and model information, they said that we would be hearing from Nancy Jones, George's wife, in the near future. Sure enough, Nancy called the next morning and placed an order. We had a nice talk and it became very clear that this poised and professional woman had her act together. It was no wonder George was enjoying a comeback. We went out of our way to make sure that the guitar was very special and that it arrived well in advance of the occasion.

After that initial interaction, we heard from Nancy and George on a more regular basis — sometimes directly and sometimes through their management or record company. Often it was to acquire more instruments for gifts or promotions. George had a lot of Martin guitars: mostly D-41s and D-45s, though there were a bunch of 28s and a few smaller-bodied 000s that had peppered his prolific career. Our conversations led eventually to a serious discussion about George's incredible musical legacy. We proposed the obvious special signature edition and George was honored. Nancy, in her own delightful way, helped to facilitate the process at every step.

At one point we thought we might see "The Possum" in the Nazareth area. Tommy Schafer and his son Tom, Jr. had built an incredible performance hall called "Rambler's Ranch" on top of the Blue Mountain ridge. With the help of some top-notch Nashville booking agents and promoters, Rambler's Ranch was bringing in some of the major country acts and, sure enough, George was on the slate. We were all set to hook up with him and Nancy when a car accident canceled the show. Nevertheless, George did recover and we forged ahead with our project.

We were a bit wary of making the guitar too fancy, but clearly George wanted a lot of pearl to glisten under the stage lights during his performances, so we compromised and focused on a D-41GJ. It had the pizzazz of a D-45 without too much over-the-top expense.

While doodling one day, I had sketched a hexagon with concave or "scalloped" edges. Given Martin's famous "scalloped" braces, the idea seemed interesting and I liked the sound of "scalloped hexagons." George did too. With the addition of a premium Engelmann spruce top, Waverly butterbean tuners, vintage-styled grained ivoroid bindings, "heart" abalone pearl bordering, and of course the

"scalloped hexagon" fingerboard with George Jones' signature in pearl, the elegant design was complete. We built the prototypes and carted them off to Nashville in the blistering July heat for their unveiling at the 2000 Summer NAMM Show. The edition of one hundred instruments sold out so quickly, we didn't know what hit us!

George asked that the charitable proceeds from the edition be donated in support of the Vanderbilt Children's Hospital, the facility that cared for him after his car accident. The only facility of its kind in the Mid-South, the Vanderbilt Children's Hospital provides comprehensive pediatric care for acute and chronic illnesses, treating nearly 100,000 young patients each year.

Of course, George loved the guitars when they finally came off the line. He bought a few of the edition guitars for himself and as gifts for some of his special friends. A few months after the dust had

It had the pizzazz of a D-45 without too much over-the-top expense.

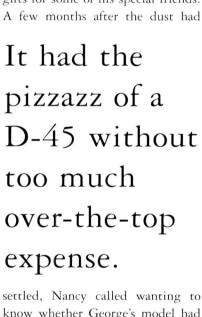

settled, Nancy called wanting to know whether George's model had done well — I told her that all one hundred instruments had evaporated as quickly as a spilled shot of vodka on a sizzling Nashville sidewalk! She laughed and yelled over to her husband: "Hey George, come on over here and say thank you to the man from Martin." The Possum meandered over to the phone and with a voice as smooth as silk he simply said: "Thanks a lot, and I really mean that!"

George Jones's life has had more triumphs and travails than a hundred jukebox songs, but from behind those Martin guitars, he continues to do what he does best — create great country music.

Above: The George Jones D-41GJ Signature Edition combines 'scalloped hexagon' fingerboard inlays with the simple elegance of Martin D-41 styling and the vintage feel of grained ivoroid bindings.

LESTER FLATT

D-28LF

Bluegrass and Brazilian

ONCE AN EDITION SIZE IS ANNOUNCED, the number produced should be strictly adhered to. This lesson was learned in the mid-nineties when a guitar collector took notice that Martin had issued separately numbered domestic and export edition labels for the Guitar Of The Month models that were introduced prior to 1995. A domestic-edition label, for example, might read 1 of 100, 2 of 100, etc. while the separate foreign-edition label would read 1 of 15, 2 of 15, etc. In 1995, Martin stopped issuing separate foreign labeling in favor of one label worldwide.

I mention this because I certainly had underestimated the demand for the Hank Williams Sr. D-28 signature model. The edition of 150 Brazilian rosewood guitars sold out very quickly with a significant waiting list, and the Martin District Sales Managers were all hollering for more. Of course, no more would ever be offered in that configuration.

It seemed an uncanny coincidence when our friend Marty Stuart called to suggest that Martin consider offering a Lester Flatt Commemorative D-28. I was immediately excited about the prospect. Lester's D-28 was very similar to Hank's, except for several challenging but unique modifications to the fingerboard and pickguard. In creating this model not only would Martin be paying tribute to one of bluegrass and country music's greatest legends; we would also be extending the availability of the highly prized Brazilian D-28.

As the owner of Lester Flatt's original D-28, Marty Stuart was happy to ship the guitar to Nazareth in exchange for some expert and long-overdue refurbishing. When the heavily insured parcel arrived, I arranged for the Repair Department to go over the guitar carefully and give it a proper cleanup and refretting.

The pickguard on Lester's D-28 was large and unwieldy, but custom-made to suit his needs. There were many oversized pickguard patterns in our possession: one for Porter Wagoner, one for Bob Shane, and several different versions for Lester Flatt. I created a digital pattern and emailed it to Pearlworks to see whether they could reproduce it with their small CNC machine. This would prove more efficient than trying to hand-cut each one. They did a beautiful job, but each pickguard still required very careful hand-fitting, especially along the treble side of the fingerboard and the leading edge of the bridge.

Prior to his long and illustrious career with Martin, Mike Longworth, historian, author, and craftsman, executed the unique inlays on Lester Flatt's original D-28. Mike began inlay work in 1955 while he was still in high school and nearly all of his early inlay jobs included the letter "L" (for Longworth) in pearl and a number designating the sequence of his work.

Right: Exacting handwork on our D-28LF edition faithfully reproduces Lester's original. Opposite page : A promo shot of Lester Flatt with his D-28, no doubt taken on stage at the Grand Ole Opry. Inset: Lester Flatt's original D-28 with custom-enlarged pickguard and Mike Longworth's inlay handiwork. Note Mike's business card glued to the back for quick reference!

Longworth was well connected to the musicians that surrounded Flatt & Scruggs; in fact his third inlay job was for Buck "Josh" Graves (their dobro player), and his fourth for Curly Seckler (their mandolin player and tenor singer). Longworth's fifth inlay project was for Lester himself, hence the "L-5" inlay at the 17th fret, indicating "Longworth Professional Inlay Job #5." To insure that there would be no misunderstandings from the Gibson Guitar Company in Nashville as a result of their L-5 archtop-guitar nomenclature, we notified Gibson's attorney about the Lester Flatt project and executed a simple agreement that clarified our usage of the L-5 inlay.

Pearlworks was also able to replicate faithfully the rectangular block of pearl bearing the name "LESTER" between the 14th and 15th frets, as well as two large white-diamond shaped inlays at the 5th and 7th frets, plus two large slotted squares at 7th and 12th frets. The relatively small edition of fifty guitars sold out as quickly as the Hank Williams model that preceded it and I was left with a feeling of great satisfaction at having paid tribute to such a musical legend. The fact remained, however, that as the workhorse of the Martin line, there would always be a demand for reissues of old Brazilian D-28s.

In creating this model not only would Martin be paying tribute to one of country music's greatest legends; we would also be extending the availability of the highly prized Brazilian D-28.

PETER ROWAN 000-18SPR

In the midnight, by the moonlight

MY AUNT CARTER has lived in the Boston area for most of her life. In her younger days, she was a very close friend of the very musical Rowan family, so it was a common occurrence in our family to receive newspaper clippings from her about the many other exciting collaborations in Peter Rowan's ongoing musical evolution. From bluegrass and folk to acoustic fusion and Tex-Mex, Peter came to personify American roots music. With his distinctive voice, refined guitar technique, and skillful songwriting, Peter helped fuel the traditional — and non-traditional — acoustic music revival for nearly forty years, both as a solo artist and as a key member for several benchmark groups including Bill Monroe and his Blue Grass Boys.

Soon after leaving Monroe, he teamed up with mandolin maestro David Grisman in the folk-rock band Earth Opera. After a stay in the rock fusion group Seatrain, Rowan joined Grisman again to sing and play bluegrass, first in Muleskinner with guitar wizard Clarence White and later in Old & In The Way, with Grateful Dead guitarist Jerry Garcia. Though both groups were short-lived, their recordings spurred a youth movement in bluegrass.

In the late seventies and through the eighties, Peter recorded and toured with his younger brothers Chris and Lorin as the Rowan Brothers, played Tex Mex rock with the notorious Free Mexican Airforce, and throughout the nineties demonstrated his musical range in a string of well-received albums culminating with a Grammy-nominated collaboration with slide master Jerry Douglas. In more recent years, Peter has toured extensively with flatpicking icon Tony Rice.

In 1999, Peter was scheduled to perform locally at the Godfrey Daniels Coffeehouse in Bethlehem. He came by Martin for a visit and later I attended the show with Martin clinician Richard Starkey. Given that Peter has been a loyal Martin player his entire career, and that he had attained such a significant status in the world of acoustic music, it didn't take long for us to gravitate toward discussions about a Peter Rowan Signature Edition.

Peter had always loved mahogany Dreadnoughts, especially the D-18S 12-fret model, but as a fingerstylist, he also loved the smaller bodied 12-fret Martins. Charles Sawtelle was one of Peter's closest friends and it was quickly decided that since Charles had played a 000 12-fret model, it would be fitting to use that body size as a memorial

of sorts to Charles. We also decided that the theme of the guitar should be based upon "Midnight Moonlight," one of Peter's legendary songs from Old & In The Way, but this required some special design consideration. Peter and I struggled with the specifications for the better part of a year.

Frustrated by the lack of progress, I enlisted the help of inlay artist Larry Robinson to suggest a motif for the fingerboard and headplate. Larry furnished rough sketches of a night sky with the moon hidden slightly behind clouds. For

> With his distinctive voice, refined guitar technique, and skillful songwriting, Peter helped fuel the traditional — and non-traditional — acoustic music revival for nearly forty years.

the fingerboard, Larry suggested a simple progression of the phases of the moon. These were great ideas, but the final artwork remained evasive and daunting. The inlays seemed to demand understatement. Black mother-of-pearl clouds were combined with a white pearl moon to create an eerie midnight moonlight effect against the black ebony sky. The completed prototypes were, of course, magnificent. Peter's expectations were exceeded and the guitars were viewed by consumers as precious works of art and sound.

I sent the press materials and photographs of the edition to my Aunt Carter and it seemed that something intangible had come full circle. For this there is an uncanny sense of satisfaction that can only be discerned by listening carefully to the subtle tonal inflections of each 000-18SPR Peter Rowan Signature Edition guitar.

Far left and above: Peter Rowan's graceful tortoise-bound mahogany 000 12-fret is artfully inlaid with the phases of the moon as fret position markers. Right: With its "Midnight Moonlight" headstock executed in white and black pearl, this guitar serves as a thoughtful tribute to Peter's great friend, Charles Sawtelle.

DEL MCCOURY D-28DM
A *tribute to one of bluegrass music's most enduring voices*

OF ALL THE MUSICAL GENRES, bluegrass is the one in which the Martin guitar is most prevalent, partly because the music is purely acoustic, but also because the Martin guitar has become so intertwined with the history and development of bluegrass music. Like the Gibson Mastertone 5-string banjo, the F-5 scroll mandolin, the string bass, and the fiddle, the Dreadnought acoustic guitar is a key ingredient in the formula for the bluegrass sound.

As a company, we have always had a strong connection and affiliation with bluegrass and bluegrass musicians. Martin's Bob Fehr regularly attends the annual International Bluegrass Music Association's "World of Bluegrass" convention in Louisville, Kentucky and he and a host of other Martin employees volunteer for an array of summer bluegrass festivals around the country.

Even though I am somewhat partial to folk, blues, and acoustic rock, I have attended enough bluegrass festivals to certainly be considered "a veteran." Thanks to David Grisman, Peter Rowan, Tony Rice, and the many other co-founders of the contemporary jazz-grass movement, I definitely caught the bluegrass bug from a different perspective at the legendary Telluride Bluegrass Festival in Colorado. I was there to represent Martin's sponsorship of the event and was privileged to spend time backstage with the likes of Johnny Cash, Bela Fleck, Sam Bush, Edgar Meyer, and Del McCoury. I came away from Telluride with a very special appreciation for Del, who had risen slowly through the ranks to assume his respected post as a bluegrass patriarch.

In February of 1966, Del's wife Jean had bought him a 1954 D-28 for his birthday. There was a Polaroid of the guitar on a bulletin board where she worked and it was for sale. She knew enough about guitars to know that Del had always wanted a D-28. Del has played that guitar for most of his career and has used it for almost all his recording sessions. He has also been seen from time to time playing another favorite, his dark-top D-18. Del's loyalty is best summed up in his own words: "After sixty-three years, I've played a lot of guitars, but nothing comes up to a Martin."

Larry Barnwell is Martin's District Sales Manager in the Pacific Northwest. A great musician in his own right, he had worked in Nashville for many years and was inextricably connected with bluegrass, not only through his vocation but also through his love of the music. Larry knew everyone. He had been friends with Bill Monroe, Chet Atkins, Lester Flatt, and Earl Scruggs. He was also very close with Del McCoury and his musical family and between Larry, Bob Fehr, and myself, our conversations gradually turned to Del and how much he deserved to be honored with a Martin signature edition.

As a member of Bill Monroe's Bluegrass Boys early in his career, Del developed a deep appreciation for the blues, both in lyrical theme and in guitar-playing style. Following this premise, we designed a simple but elegant ebony fingerboard, decorated with position dots of blue lapis, each trimmed with a thin ring of pearl. The blues theme continued with lapis-inlaid ebony bridge pins.

Tonally, the most significant feature of Del's D-28DM Signature Edition guitar was the Adirondack spruce soundboard, adorned with a simple vintage "Style 18" rosette, with a thin band of blue Paua shell as the center ring. Combined with the warmth of East Indian rosewood back and sides, the D-28DM prototype was so powerful that it immediately took the place of Del's older Martins — and everyone knows how hard it is to outperform an old Martin!

One hundred and fifteen orders were taken for the edition — that's 115 very serious bluegrass guitars. It's a fitting tribute for a man with such clear integrity and talent. Del stipulated that the charitable proceeds from the sale of each of his signature guitars be donated in support of the American Heart Association.

Above: Del McCoury christens his signature-model prototype on stage at Nashville's Ryman Auditorium in July of 2002.
Below: Adirondack red spruce and a thin band of Paua shell grace the vintage-styled soundboard of the D-28DM.

GRAND OLE OPRY HDO
New techniques to honor one of America's enduring musical legacies

MARTIN HAS HAD A LONG AND COLORFUL HISTORY with Gaylord Entertainment. Late in 1971, as the Opryland Theme Park was nearing completion, Martin entered into a sponsorship agreement with Gaylord to underwrite The Martin Bluegrass Theater. A remote log-cabin structure was purchased, disassembled, moved, and reconstructed with some modifications for the theater's stage. Open benches capable of seating about three or four hundred people arced in a graduated radius up from the stage.

The Martin Bluegrass Theater was a popular venue at the park with about seven packed performances every day. Heading up the show were Russ and Becky Jeffers with their band Smokey Mountain Sunshine. They were often joined by many of the legendary members of the Grand Ole Opry like Porter Wagoner, Roy Acuff, Grandpa Jones, and Charlie Collins. Martin guitars were the official acoustic guitars of Opryland and though they were not exclusively played, there were a lot of Martins in use. We kept the instrument cage well stocked with an assortment of models that the various musicians could sign out for their performances. Of course Russ Jeffers was a Martin player and fan, and he talked about Martin guitars during every show.

But all good things must eventually come to an end. Due to decreasing revenues at the park, Opryland was closed on December 31, 1997. As a matter of record, the very last performance at the park was at the Martin Bluegrass Theater. Russ and Becky played "Rocky Top" to an emotional crowd of employees and fans. Soon afterwards, the grounds were bulldozed in preparation for the construction of

Opry Mills, a high-end shopping outlet. Our sponsorship gradually came to its logical conclusion. It fell under my job responsibility to inventory the instruments on loan to the park and to make arrangements to bring them back to Nazareth.

There were a few problems. Responsibility for the instruments had changed many times through the years, resulting in the mismanagement of the Martin instruments. Many were missing and the ones that were accounted for were in very bad condition. The process of rectifying this situation was time consuming, but it gave Martin a bit of bargaining power. Toward that end, we suggested that our companies look for a way to collaborate in the creation of a Grand Ole Opry 75th Anniversary edition.

The various powers that be responded well to the idea and soon I found myself working directly with Rusty Summerville of Gaylord's Art Department on initial designs for a model. My idea was to develop artwork for the famous WSM 650 radio microphone for the headstock of the guitar. For the fingerboard, the stylized "Grand Ole Opry" red letters from the white placards that appeared on the Opry Stage would create the perfect illusion. Rusty and I consternated over the design, sending computer images back and forth until, after much refining, the finalized inlay drawings for Larry Sifel and Jeff Harding of Pearlworks were completed. Pearlworks added their valuable input as well while digitizing the image and Rusty came through with the last-minute addition of the pearl inlaid audio cable, snaking with realism around the mike stand, creating a shimmering contrast against the ebony headplate.

Above: This beautiful handpainted sign hung at the entrance to the General Jackson steamship in Opryland Theme Park.

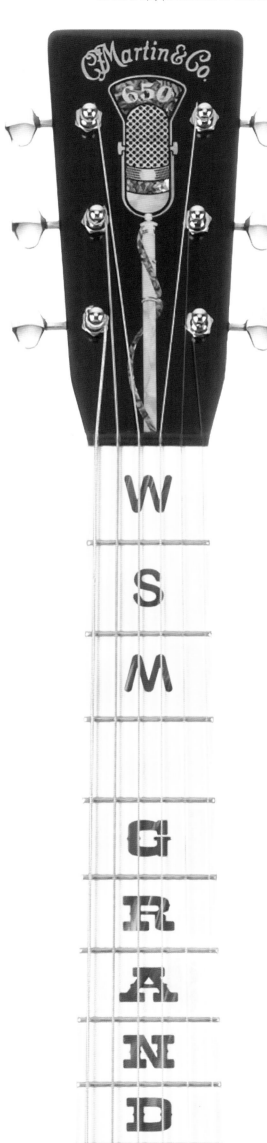

We sent out ebony fingerboards for inlay with red pearlescent letters spelling out "WSM GRAND OLE OPRY" across the vertical length of the fingerboard and "1925–2000" at the final fret. The lettering was recreated in the style of the original stage placards, but when they were complete, the letters just didn't look right against black. A white background was clearly needed.

Tim Teel in the R&D Department was working on an assortment of new materials and I sought his help in solving my fingerboard dilemma. He had some 1/4″ thick sheets of both Micarta® and Corian® at his bench and he had them processed into fingerboards so that we could see how effectively the frets could be seated. Though both were workable, the Corian® was lily white with a waxy texture and appearance. The Micarta® on the other hand was elegant and creamy, almost ivory in color, with a smooth matt finish. It seemed an inspired choice — one reminiscent of the genuine ivory fingerboards on many of the pre-1850 Martin instruments built by our founder. It quickly became clear that this material, in its black coloration, would take on increasing significance as a viable replacement for ebony, especially on Martin's more economically priced instruments.

Based upon Martin's Style 28 "herringbone" Dreadnought with scalloped braces, the HDO Opry guitars were limited to no more than 650 individually numbered instruments, each bearing a pair of photographic interior labels that depicted the famous red brick facade of the Ryman Auditorium where Opry radio broadcasts originated and remained for more than thirty of its colorful seventy-five-year history.

The stage of the Grand Ole Opry has presented such musical legends as Hank Williams Sr., Jimmie Rodgers, Ernest Tubb, and Lester Flatt as well as all today's superstars including Marty Stuart, George Jones, Dolly Parton, Willie Nelson, and Johnny Cash. It is not surprising that more than forty members of the Grand Ole Opry purchased these anniversary models, acknowledging the close role Martin has played (and continues to play) as the guitar of choice for so many of Nashville's greatest artists, and paying tribute at the same time to the Opry, one of America's most enduring musical legacies.

The Opry placard's stylistic letters were faithfully recreated and inlaid in red pearloid.
Other appointments of the guitar pay tribute to Martin's legendary herringbone D-28.

ELVIS PRESLEY
The King's legendary "ELVI" D-18

VERY EARLY IN HIS CAREER, before he had attained any degree of fame, Elvis Presley took his inexpensive beat-up old guitar down to the O. K. Houck Music Company on Union Street (in Memphis we believe) and traded it in for a 1942 Martin D-18 (Serial #80221). Houck's gave him $8 trade-in on the old guitar, which Elvis had used to learn on, then promptly put it out back with the garbage. Of course, the Martin was also "used" but it must have been in reasonable condition. Elvis paid $175 for the guitar and is purported to have been embarrassed at having made such an extravagant purchase, but since this was to be his profession, he surely rationalized the purchase as a critical tool of his trade.

Many photographs show Elvis with the guitar. Originally, self-adhesive metallic block letters spelled "E-L-V-I-S" along the bottom left bout of the Martin, but somewhere along the line the "S" was lost leaving "ELVI." Ever since, the famous instrument has become known as the "ELVI" guitar.

Elvis played his D-18 acoustic guitar exclusively between 1954 and 1956, and also on the legendary Sun Sessions recordings produced by Sam Phillips. He recorded most of his early hits on the Martin, including "That's All Right" and "Blue Moon of Kentucky," and used it for all his early concert performances.

According to Jim Jaworowitz, memorabilia consultant to Graceland and Christie's, the Martin (and the discarded learner guitar) are the only two guitars Elvis Presley played that are not currently owned by Graceland. The guitar parted ways with Elvis in 1956 when it was sold to a neighbor and fan who owned it for thirty-five years. For many of those years, the D-18 was displayed in the north wing of the Country Music Hall Of Fame, with a photograph showing Elvis performing on stage with the guitar. The Hall Of Fame considered the instrument one of the most significant items that they have ever had on exhibit.

Seeing an obvious opportunity, Bob Brown, owner of the Red Baron's auction house in Atlanta, Georgia, purchased the guitar and placed it on pre-auction display at Turner Broadcasting's CNN Center with an array of loaned Martin artefacts, old photographs, and some of the old forms and tools that no doubt linked with the guitar's original construction.

Red Baron organized and conducted the subsequent auction of the D-18 in Atlanta, Georgia on October 5, 1991. The guitar sold for the sum of $180,000 to an unnamed antiques dealer and collector in London. Since then the D-18 has changed hands several times. Martin had the opportunity to photograph the ELVI guitar when it returned to Nazareth for some restoration work in the mid- nineteen-nineties.

Among the many Martins that Elvis owned were his leather-covered D-28 performance guitar (above left) and his famous D-18 ELVI guitar (above right), missing its "S."

DION 000-CBD

The Wanderer

BILL BUSH IS ARGUABLY ONE OF THE COUNTRY'S MOST knowledgeable experts on both early rock 'n' roll and also the folk-music revival. As a Buddy Holly historian and a close observer of the evolution of The Kingston Trio amongst many others, Bill is often called upon to write magazine articles and liner notes about these and other musical sensations of the 1950s.

Bill is also a serious aficionado and collector of Martin guitars. In the late-eighties he visited the factory and shared his ideas about the direction of Martin advertising. As the head of his own advertising firm, Bill was in a unique position to understand the guitar market, perhaps even better than the people at Martin. At the time I was heading up the in-house advertising effort and I sought Bill's advice and expertise in conceptualizing ad headlines and body copy.

In keeping with his role as a music historian and journalist, Bill Bush had also become good friends with Dion DiMucci. For over forty years, Dion has been a major recording artist, rock 'n' roll pioneer and inspiration for scores of singers, songwriters, and guitarists — including Bruce Springsteen, Bob Dylan, and Paul Simon.

Dion began his career in 1958 as lead singer of Dion and The Belmonts, recording such classics as "I Wonder Why" and "Teenager In Love." Going solo in 1960, he again launched a long run of top-ten hits including "Runaround Sue," "The Wanderer," "Ruby Baby," and "Donna, The Prima Donna." Shifting from pop to acoustic blues and folk in the mid-sixties, he once more scored a major hit with the release of "Abraham, Martin and John" in 1968.

Throughout the seventies and eighties, Dion continued to tour and record, immersing himself in contemporary gospel music, culminating with a Grammy award nomination in 1983 and his subsequent induction into the Rock And Roll Hall Of Fame. Today he still records and tours, and remains a significant influence on American music.

Throughout all Dion's recorded work, Martin guitars have been an important mainstay, including a D-18, several D-28s, and a 12-fret D-35S. At our prompting, Bill Bush notified Dion that we were interested in honoring him with a signature-model collaboration. Dion was deeply appreciative and jumped into the project with great enthusiasm. He was not content, however, to simply rehash tradition. He had definite ideas about what his guitar needed to be, and after trying many Martin models, he ordered an SP000C-16E model to test out in his studio.

The small-bodied 000 confirmed Dion's conviction that he wanted a guitar that would work well both on stage and in the studio. Accordingly, he felt it critical that the instrument have acoustic electric capabilities and a cutaway to access the upper frets. For him, the 000 size offered great Martin acoustic sound for performances, and evenly balanced tonality for recording. He also thought that black was "definitely a very cool color for a rock 'n' roll guitar!"

"As a kid, I only had two goals in life – to date Marilyn Monroe and to own a Martin guitar."

Bill Bush was working on a number of projects with Dion and used his occasional visits to advise him and communicate with Martin about many of the design details for the signature model. Symbolizing Dion's deep religious faith, two small pearl doves were created to adorn the wings of the bridge. Designs for the skyline headplate inlay had been completed long before the tragic events of September 11, and had originally included 'The Wanderer' rather than Dion's signature. After the tragedy, Dion asked that "The Wanderer" inscription above the spire of the Empire State Building be replaced with his signature to signify his support and love of New York City, his hometown. "The Wanderer" remained an important element, in mother-of-pearl at the end of the fingerboard.

The prototypes were completed and one was shipped to Dion as Christmas of 2001 was approaching. Dion called on the phone. The line was busy, but he left one of his classic answering machine messages.

Yo Dick! This is Dion Dion Dion — this isn't Paul Simon This is Dion!

I got the guitar, and ah, I must have written two songs already. I got so inspired. Its beautiful. What could I tell ya. I feel like... I don't know the words. I feel like — The Prince Of Poetry — The King of Choruses — The Royalty of Rock 'n' Roll — The Baron of Ballads — The Sultan of Swing (Oh no, that's that other guy...)

Hey, it's gorgeous. It sounds... It's just... I didn't even use the preamp or anything. I just plugged it in. And acoustically it has a beautiful sound. It's just total total total total totally, wow! I'm flabbergasted.

It's a good Xmas, ain't it? Stay well. I thank you.

God Bless!

The charitable proceeds from the project were donated in support of The SOS Children's Village in Coconut Creek, Florida, a children's charity that provides homes, parents, families, and support services for children in foster care. In total fifty-seven of the Dion guitars were made — 1957 was the year his first hits started to shake the foundations of American music. Once the guitars got out into the marketplace, people started to realize how cool they were — just like the man himself...

Yo!

Left: Dion with the prototype of 000-CBD. Above: The full view of Dion's signature edition reveals an ebony midnite sky over the New York City skyline.

THE KINGSTON TRIO

A three-piece edition celebrates the group's unique place in music history

THE ORIGINAL KINGSTON TRIO was formed in 1957 by Bob Shane, Nick Reynolds, and Dave Guard. With their acoustic guitars and banjos, they revolutionized and reawakened American popular music, paving the way for a broader acceptance of bluegrass, blues, country, and other indigenous American genres. The release of "Tom Dooley" in 1958 marked the beginning of the folk music revival and set the stage for Bob Dylan, Joan Baez, Peter, Paul & Mary, and the entire protest-music movement of the sixties.

Late in 1995, Bill Bush informed us that the fortieth anniversary of the founding of The Kingston Trio was fast approaching. With Bill's contacts and guidance, we embarked on a collaborative effort with group founder Bob Shane to create a three-piece limited-edition set of

Kingston Trio signature instruments: a six-string Martin D-28, a four-string 0-18T tenor, and a long-neck five-string banjo. The project seemed especially pertinent given that few other groups have had such a profound impact upon the course of American acoustic music.

Since Martin had abandoned banjo making with the sale of Vega in the early eighties, Greg and Janet Deering of Deering Banjos were enlisted to produce the Kingston Trio Vega-styled long-neck banjo. The 25-fret neck, originally suggested to Vega by Pete Seeger, facilitated easy key changes to suit the vocalist, and soon became the "workhorse banjo" of virtually every major folk group.

Back at Martin, we modified lettering from Bill Bush's boxed set liner notes to produce the Kingston Trio mother-of-pearl inlays that

Above: The Kingston Trio Limited Edition Set of Three Instruments: left to right the 0-18T tenor, the Vega long-neck folk model banjo and the D-28KT.

would grace the fingerboards of all three instruments. Each of the instruments featured a numbered interior label personally signed by Chris Martin, Trio members Bob Shane, Nick Reynolds, and George Grove, and former member John Stewart. A memorial to deceased members Dave Guard and Roger Gambill was also included on the label. The instruments were offered for sale as an unbroken set of three and the edition of thirty-four sets that were made remain very rare and highly prized by their owners.

With 2003 marking the forty-fifth anniversary of the founding of The Kingston Trio, Martin revisited the project to pay special tribute to guitarist and group leader Bob Shane with the introduction of the D-28KTBS Signature Edition. Bob Shane's driving rhythm guitar was always at the heart of the Trio's sound. A physically powerful player, Bob has always led the group with a solid right-on-the-note rhythm. Many regard Bob Shane as one of the best acoustic rhythm players of the folk era. His guitar of choice has always been the Martin D-28 and his use of the instrument exposed generations of new guitar players to Martin guitars.

The Kingston Trio performs to this day, driven by Bob Shane's leadership and energy. Longtime Trio stalwarts Bob Haworth and George Grove (also Martin players) complete the group, occasionally joined by Trio veterans John Stewart and Nick Reynolds for special concert reunions.

The Kingston Trio was a catalyst for an entire social and cultural phenomenon that affected our musical tastes and our social conscience. The group will always hold a special place in American musical history and in Martin's unique evolution as an instrument maker.

Joan's original 1929 0-45 (Serial Number #39346). Joan has performed and recorded with this guitar throughout most of her career.

JOAN BAEZ
0-45JB
An old and valuable guitar harbors a secret

ONE AFTERNOON, I WAS FLIPPING THROUGH one of the guitar magazines and noticed that Joan Baez was pictured with another brand of guitar. I was horrified: she had been playing her 1929 Martin 0-45 guitar throughout her entire career. I called her office immediately to find out why she wasn't playing her old Martin.

Nancy, Joan's assistant, mentioned that someone from another guitar company had told Joan that her Martin was worth more than $100,000 and that she was crazy to keep it on the road with her. Apparently she was then offered one of the competition's guitar models. Heeding that advice, she retired the Martin to her bedroom and started touring with the non-Martin model. I was distressed.

A week later Joan confirmed the story but added that, after thirty years of constant use, her old Martin was much the worse for wear. The fingerboard had been poorly replaced and some of the inlays were missing altogether. There were some hairline cracks in the sides and the action was high. I offered to restore the guitar for her at no charge and several weeks later a heavily insured carton arrived at the factory, containing the legendary and precious guitar.

Shortly after Joan's guitar was unpacked and thoroughly diagnosed my phone rang. It was Milt Hess Jr. in the Repair Department. He was upset and wanted to see me right away at his bench.

"You won't believe this," he said. He turned on a small light that he had placed inside the body of the guitar and handed me an inspection mirror. I took a look.

There, on the underbelly of the top, the bold words were haphazardly scrawled:

"Too bad you are a Communist"

The statement was legible only with use of the mirror, which meant that someone had purposefully and clumsily written the words in backwards. It occurred to me that Joan might have had the instrument serviced during the Vietnam War years, probably by someone who seriously objected to Joan's politics. Milt was worried that she might think that someone from Martin had done this. He asked that I call her with the news.

When I reached her on the phone, I asked whether she was sitting down. I wasn't sure how she was going to take this. I related the whole story and when the word "communist" rolled off my tongue, there was an uneasy silence, then a

Below: A special "reversed" interior label explaining the unusual story of Joan's guitar was affixed to the underside of the top, decipherable only with a luthier's inspection mirror.

Joan Baez's original 0-45 guitar had undergone a lot of wear and tear, and at the beginning of her collaboration with Martin, she shipped her priceless guitar back to the factory for some restoration work. When the interior of Joan's guitar was being carefully examined with an inspection mirror by Martin repair technicians, it was discovered that on the underside of the top soundboard, there was clearly written in pencil:

"Too bad you are a communist"

Apparently, Joan had had the instrument worked on during the peak of anti-war controversy. The workers in the Martin repair department wanted to make especially certain that Joan knew that this was done by a previous repair person, and not by anyone at Martin.

It turns out that when Joan was notified about this, she was amused and somewhat honored to be thought of as a communist in the post cold-war era.

spontaneous burst of laughter. Joan laughed for several minutes. She thought the story was hilarious.

The restoration of the guitar went beautifully. Before returning the completed instrument to her, I took very careful measurements and photographs and in the weeks that followed I proposed a Limited Edition Joan Baez Signature Model Martin guitar, with royalties that would support Bread & Roses, the West Coast music charity that her sister Mimi Farina had founded. Joan loved the idea and we proceeded with a prototype that drew its inspiration from her 0-45. As the prototype neared completion, I awoke in the middle of the night with an idea. Why not make a special label for the underside of the top, readable only with an inspection mirror, that told the story in short order, complete with the "Too bad you are a Communist" punchline.

Martin made only fifty-nine of these very special guitars, an edition size based on 1959, the year that Joan Baez came onto the scene at the Newport Folk Festival. The entire edition sold out immediately. Of course, Joan requested the number-one instrument in the edition and she purchased several others for close musical friends, including singer-songwriter Dar Williams.

Eventually, Joan's tour brought her to the Ballroom at the Bellview Hotel in Philadelphia. I met her there. She was playing the number-one guitar and halfway through her performance she stopped. Holding the guitar proudly up for the audience, she spent ten minutes telling the entire story. The audience roared.

I understand that when Joan is bold enough to travel with her precious Martin guitars, she always tells that story with great animation and pride.

Below: Detail of Joan's signature in pearl, plus the elegance of the vintage Style-45 appointments.
Right: Joan after a performance at the Belleview in Philadelphia, with her signature model.
Martin's torch inlay pattern graces the headstock.

Dear Dick,

This is the most beautiful guitar
I've ever laid my hands on. I'm
speechless –

I'll be touring with it, loving it
cleaning it, and making music with
it for many audiences to come.
          Thank you all at Martin
                    Joan.

(P.S. Too bad I'm a Communist.)

HDN
Negatively 4th Street

ANY CONVERSATION ABOUT MUSIC in the past four decades has to include Bob Dylan. Like Elvis Presley and The Beatles, his influence is so pervasive it is simply impossible to measure.

As a fervent Dylan fan, I had certainly followed every evolution of his music and career. In fact I delayed my employment at Martin by one day in order to attend one of his concerts. There were stories floating around Martin that he had visited the factory in the sixties. Supposedly he had flown into the Allentown airport and taken a cab to the plant to have his Martin guitar diagnosed and adjusted, then he quickly flew back out.

In any case, Bob Dylan has owned and played many Martin guitars throughout his incredible musical journey. It's only fair to say that he has also played other brands of guitars to suit his specific need at any given moment. For certain, he owned some Dreadnoughts in the early days, most likely a D-18 and D-28, and he has often been seen with smaller-bodied Martins such as the 00-18 that he held during a photo session for the cover of *Acoustic Guitar* magazine.

For several years, Cesar Diaz was Bob's guitar technician and amplifier specialist. Cesar was also a great player and joined in with Bob's band for a time, during which he often visited Martin to stock up on plenty of strings and to acquire a variety of stock and custom guitars for the tour. A few HD-28s and an OM-28 Perry Bechtel were purchased. Bob took a special liking to one of the HDs and played it for several years — or at least long enough for a dark stain to develop at the edge of the guitar where he rested his leather-jacketed arm while playing. This HD-28 was used during the performance that was recorded for *MTV Unplugged*.

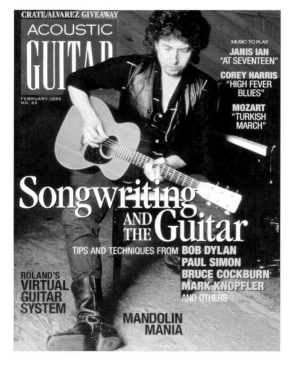

Through a good bit of custom experimentation, it became clear that Dylan liked the full-sized Dreadnoughts with full-thickness necks and bright Engelmann spruce tops. In reverence to Jimmie Rodgers, Bob had a particular appreciation for slotted headstocks.

There is a "Tex Fletcher" Dreadnought in the Martin Museum with thin block lettering on the fingerboard. Cesar conveyed to me that Bob liked that style of lettering, so I drafted a special "Bob Dylan" fingerboard that was subsequently inlaid by David Nichols of Custom Pearl Inlay. The fingerboard found its place on a Custom Dreadnought that Cesar delivered to Bob, but by the time it was completed, Cesar's role in the band was changing. Eventually, Cesar stopped working with Dylan altogether and there was some question whether the Custom Dreadnought remained in the corral of Dylan instruments.

Musicians close to Dylan were also playing Martin guitars. G. E. Smith joined several legs of the tour with his battle-scarred D-18. George Harrison borrowed the Perry Bechtel OM-28 for a televised Dylan Tribute Concert at Madison Square Garden along with Eric Clapton, who played his prewar 000-42. Bob played his leather-stained herringbone. Rick Okasic of The Cars was represented by Bob's management and he ended up in possession of a fancy pearl-inlaid Custom OM with gloss black lacquer that had initially been ordered for Dylan. In the later part of the nineties, Larry Campbell joined the band with his HD-28V.

As the new millennium approached, *Acoustic Guitar* magazine began planning for their tenth anniversary. The editors put together a promotion wherein most of the key acoustic-guitar manufacturers were invited to contribute a matching pair of special guitars that would incorporate the magazine's tenth-anniversary logo in pearl. We were asked to "push the envelope" with respect to the design, and having just completed the HDO Grand Ole Opry prototypes, I thought it would be interesting to utilize the same ivory-colored Micarta® fingerboard on our herringbone Dreadnought offering. As the design evolved, we added an ivory-colored bridge and headplate. When the idea of black lacquer emerged, it became clear that this was going to be a very bold visual statement. In conversations with Danny Brown, the Martin craftsman that was building the actual prototypes, it occurred to us that the instrument was starting to look like a black-and-white photo negative. We embraced this notion and followed it through to its logical conclusion. The resulting two guitars were most unusual and soon the guitar appeared in the pages of *Acoustic Guitar*.

A very capable and amiable Tom Morrongello had assumed the role of guitar technician in Dylan's camp. It wasn't very long before Tom called back to say that Bob had seen the "Negative" guitar in the magazine and he wanted one. The only problem was that only two were made — one was a promotional giveaway and the other was a permanent part of the magazine's anniversary collection.

I explained this to Tom and since both guitars were unavailable, we offered to make another pair for Bob. The tenth-anniversary logo was replaced with the Don McLean altered torch inlay pattern and Engelmann spruce was selected for the sounding board. Naturally, we had high hopes for a Bob Dylan Signature Edition, but it was much more important to try to produce instruments worthy of Bob Dylan's approval and use.

The guitars were completed in time for the release of Dylan's inspired *Love & Theft* CD and the beginning of the Neverending Tour. Double cream-colored pickguards were added at Bob's request. We were thrilled that Bob was using the instruments but it became quite clear that he had no real desire or need to endorse any product, nor would he ever be willing to obligate himself exclusively with a particular brand. Nonetheless, the concept of the "Negative" guitar was too good to let pass. Dubbing it the HDN, new final prototypes were completed and introduced at the Nashville NAMM Show in July of 2002. In spite of its "negativity," many thought the guitar was the most striking instrument on the show floor and consequently, a respectable but limited edition of 135 instruments was produced.

Above: Bob Dylan appeared on the cover of the February 1998 issue of *Acoustic Guitar* magazine with a Martin 00-18.
Opposite Left: The striking HDN "Negative" model with color-reversed features much like a photographic negative.
Opposite Right: A custom 14-fret slotted head Dreadnought with "Tex Fletcher" style letters commissioned by Cesar Diaz for Bob Dylan.

55

Woody Guthrie liked smaller-bodied guitars, sometimes with mahogany tops and sometimes with spruce. Though not exclusive to any brand, he owned a lot of Martin guitars through the years — mostly 0, 00, or 000 size — this one is likely to be a 14-fret 00-17 or 00-18.

WOODY GUTHRIE 000-18WG
"This world is your world. Take it easy, but take it!"

IN THE SUMMER OF 1998, Arlo visited the Martin factory with the old 00-17 Martin that his father Woody Guthrie had given him as a child. The instrument was in very rough condition and in the process of getting the guitar reconditioned, discussions about the potential for a Woody Guthrie commemorative model began.

Considered one of the most influential folk musicians of all time, Woody Guthrie's music and controversial politics were influenced by his own experiences as a migrant farm worker. His songs include classics such as "This Land Is Your Land" reflecting his concern about class conflict, union issues and the American West. He impacted some of this country's greatest songwriters including Pete Seeger, Leadbelly, Bob Dylan, Bruce Springsteen, and many others. Woody died of Huntington's Disease in 1967 and was inducted post-humously into the Rock And Roll Hall Of Fame in 1988.

Woody had owned literally hundreds of guitars throughout his career, many of them Martins. He gravitated toward more affordable smaller-bodied 0, 00, and 000 mahogany guitars, and he would often give his instruments away to aspiring musicians along the way. Irreverently, he often wrote or drew on his instruments. Perhaps one of his more famous assertions was: "This Machine Kills Fascists," a quote which Woody painted or carved on most of the guitars he owned.

In researching the models that Woody had owned and played, I spent a full day at The Guthrie Foundation rummaging through the Woody Guthrie Archives in New York City. The Foundation is run by Harold Levanthal, Woody's friend and manager, and by Nora Guthrie, Woody's daughter and Arlo's older sister. The archives were well organized and very thorough. I was able to find several great photographs of Woody with his Martin guitars, two of which were taken by Woody's friend Seema Weatherwax in California.

After much discussion with Arlo, we decided that in spite of the fact that Woody probably owned more Style-15 and 17 mahogany-topped Martins than he did Style 18s, it would serve Woody's memory best to use the 000-18 as the basis for the commemorative guitar. In discussions with Nora we wrestled with how to incorporate Woody's irreverence without spoiling the project or being too inappropriate. We settled on an interior label in bold backwards lettering, "This Guitar Kills Fascists," neatly concealed but ever present on the underside of the soundboard. Arlo and Nora Guthrie joined Harold Levanthal and Chris Martin in signing the numbered edition label for each guitar. A third label replicated a self-portrait sketch of Woody and his guitar with the artist's memorable words, "This world is your world. Take it easy, but take it!"

Left: A top detail of the Woody Guthrie
Limited Edition 000-18WG Commemorative.
Below: One of Woody's personally carved 000-18
guitars that resurfaced in 2002
as part of the estate of Eddie Albert.

"I am out to sing songs that will prove to you that this is your world and that if it has hit you pretty hard and knocked you for a dozen loops, no matter what color, what size you are, how you are built, I am out to sing the songs that make you take pride in yourself and in your work."

woody guthrie

Being very much aware of Woody's sentiment about material possessions, Nora and I discussed the possibility of passing one of the prototypes from person to person without ownership. The idea centered around an interior label that would instruct the person in possession to relinquish the guitar to the next person after keeping it for just one day. As much as we liked this idea, we imagined that the guitar would very quickly vanish. Perhaps the idea would have worked in Woody's era.

The charitable proceeds from the sale of the Woody Guthrie guitars were evenly split between The Guthrie Center, providing a place to bring together individuals for spiritual service as well as cultural and educational exchange, and the Woody Guthrie Foundation, whose mission it remains to preserve and perpetuate the legacy of folk musician Woody Guthrie.

When 000-18WG models reached completion, Nora, Arlo, and Jody Guthrie each received one of the guitars, a fitting memento and tribute to their father, whose individuality and spirit left an indelible mark on American music and culture.

SINGOUT! 00-17SO!
The hammer of justice — the bell of freedom

SING OUT! magazine has long been a champion of traditional and contemporary folk and acoustic music and has now become the longest continuously published folk music magazine in the world.

Through more than five decades, Martin and *Sing Out!* have maintained a close, almost symbiotic relationship. Coincidentally, *Sing Out!* moved its offices to Bethlehem, Pennsylvania, in the early eighties, just a stone's throw from Martin's headquarters in Nazareth.

In 1990, Martin recognized *Sing Out!*'s fortieth anniversary with a special edition collaboration of forty 000-18SO! guitars. Following

that success, forty-five HD-28SO! 12-fret models were offered in 1995. Shortly thereafter, Martin was inspired to re-introduce the HD-28S to the list of stock-model offerings.

The year of the millennium marked the fiftieth anniversary of *Sing Out!*, and something special was in order. The very first issue of *Sing Out!* magazine was published in May of 1950. The cover featured the music and lyrics to a then little-known song by Pete Seeger and Lee Hays of the politically controversial folk foursome The Weavers. A little more than a decade later, Peter, Paul & Mary's recording of "The Hammer Song" (renamed "If I Had A Hammer") became a defining anthem for the exploding "folk boom" of the early sixties.

Working closely with *Sing Out!* executive director/editor Mark Moss and *Sing Out!* friends Roger Dietz and Carl Apter, we envisioned a small-bodied 00-17SO! that would draw its inspiration from both the song that graced the cover of that first *Sing Out!* issue as well as the vocal group that helped birth it. The fingerboard inlays were designed to incorporate the symbols within the three verses of "The Hammer Song." A laborer's arm bearing the "hammer of justice," the liberty "bell of freedom," and musical notes depicting "a song about the love between my brothers and my sisters." The *Sing Out!* logo marked the octave fret and "1950–2000" was positioned in pearl above the final fret.

Once again, Jeff and Larry at Pearlworks jumped in to lend their support. As big fans of both *Sing Out!* and The Weavers, they took the project on as their personal challenge, but the first round of prototype fingerboards came in with inlays that were significantly larger and out of scale with the artwork that I had created. Reluctantly, I called and asked that the inlays be redone and scaled to a more tasteful size. Executed in various shades of abalone, white pearl, gold pearl, and agoya shell, the final inlay designs were striking, and in keeping with the previous *Sing Out!* editions, a subtle ebony neck heel cap was inlaid with the *Sing Out!* "exclamation mark" in mother-of-pearl.

As the icing on the cake, Mark Moss arranged for the three surviving members of the Weavers (Pete Seeger, Fred Hellerman, and Ronnie Gilbert) to join Chris Martin in signing the numbered-edition label, and the fourth member of the group, Lee Hays, who had passed away in 1981, was memorialized. A second interior label replicated the May, 1950 cover artwork of Issue No. 1 of *Sing Out!* Most appropriately, the charitable proceeds from the 00-17SO! edition were donated in support of the nonprofit *Sing Out!* organization, with a mission to "preserve the cultural diversity and heritage of traditional folk music, to support creators of new folk music from all countries and cultures, and to encourage the practice of folk music as a living phenomenon."

The *Sing Out!* fiftieth annniversary edition was a complete success. In fact the model was so well received that Martin soon revived several 17-Series models back into the line. Another nice ripple effect of the project was that Weavers guitarist Fred Hellerman, one of the undisputed patriarchs of folk music, called to arrange a visit to Martin. He brought with him his old 00-28G, a somewhat obscure Brazilian rosewood wide-necked classical guitar, braced for nylon or gut strings (hence the "G"), but which Fred had liked to use with silk and steels. Time and the unintended extra tension of steel strings had taken an extreme toll on the guitar, so Fred had brought it back for some refurbishment. The guitar served Fred through the entire span of his career. Now in fully restored condition, it stands as a symbol of The Weaver's impact upon American musical culture.

GODFREY DANIELS

MY CONNECTION WITH THIS INTIMATE LITTLE FOLK CLUB first goes all the way back to 1976 when Godfrey's first opened. I had just returned from two years in Stowe, Vermont as an art teacher and found a thriving counter-culture community on Bethlehem's south side. Godfrey's was at the heart of this scene and soon I was an occasional host of Sunday night open mikes.

Founded by folk musician Dave Fry, new-age cook Cindy Dinsmore, and a small circle of friends, the coffee house focused on fostering contemporary acts whose styles are rooted in traditional music. Without losing sight of their vision, Godfrey's successfully blossomed into a well-respected venue on the East Coast music scene, hosting a remarkable and continuing array of folk legends. After twenty-five years, Godfrey's continues as a warm hearted, open-minded "listening room", where Martin guitars have always rung out and delicious treats and coffee have always been served. In celebration of the twenty-fifth anniversary and in honor of their contributions to the arts, Martin collaborated with long-time artistic director Dave Fry in the creation of a 000-16RGD Godfrey Daniels Anniversary Edition guitar.

This simply appointed, long-scale, 14-fret rosewood 000 was designed to appeal to up-and-coming acoustic musicians. The fingerboard is inlaid with a pair of eighth notes from the Godfrey's logo between the 4th and 5th frets, "GODFREY DANIELS" is inlaid between the 11th and 13th frets, and "Est. 1976" adorns the end of the fingerboard.

The numbered-edition label bears the signatures of founder Dave Fry and Chris Martin. An adjacent label is signed by some of the respected performers that continue to grace the stage of the hundred-seat venue: Norman Blake, John Hammond, Chris Smither, Utah Phillips, John Gorka, Rosalie Sorrels, and co-founder Cindy Dinsmore.

Limited to only one hundred instruments, this is truly a celebration of what Martin does, inspired by a group of friends who have become a significant beacon to performers and fans of folk, blues, country, and a variety of other cultural genres.

Top: The 00-17SP! SingOut! model commemorates the fiftieth anniversary of *Sing Out!* magazine and The Weaver's pertinent "Hammer Song."
Bottom: The 000-16RGD model celebrated the twenty-fifth anniversary of Godfrey Daniels, one of the East Coast's most significant folk clubs.

ELIZABETH COTTEN 00-18CTN

A modest woman with the power of a Freight Train

WHILE WORKING WITH RICHARD JOHNSTON and Jim Washburn, I became reacquainted with the recordings of Elizabeth Cotten and her significant contribution to American folk music. I was certainly aware of the song "Freight Train," though I probably would have attributed it to bluesman Taj Mahal. That was the version I knew, though versions by Pete Seeger, Mike Seeger, Peter, Paul & Mary, and many others had been recorded.

But it was Elizabeth "Libba" Cotton who created the fingerstyle anthem that so defined the folk revival of the sixties. She wrote the song at the incredible age of eleven. Eighty years later she was recognized with a Grammy for her achievement. Learning the "Freight Train" song had become a prerequisite, a rite of passage for anyone aspiring to be a folk singer. To top it off for Martin, Elizabeth Cotten was faithful to the 00-18 that she used in performances and recordings throughout the full span of her professional career.

I wasn't sure whom to contact concerning an Elizabeth Cotten commemorative edition, but after a few phone calls I found myself speaking with Mike Seeger. He certainly was the right person. He relayed to me the incredible series of events that enabled her talent to be discovered. Libba was working as a department-store clerk in Washington, DC when she helped a lost child reunite with a very worried mother. That child was Mike's sister, Peggy. As a result of that chance encounter Mrs. Seeger hired Libba to do housework, and the Seeger family soon discovered her guitar virtuosity and the wealth of folk songs that she knew. Mike, Peggy, and their cousin Pete Seeger all helped bring Libba's music to the public. Mike produced all three of her Folkways albums.

Libba was naturally left-handed. The sole guitar in the Cotten household belonged to her older brother who was right-handed. For practical reasons, Libba was forced to learn to play the guitar (and banjo for that matter) upside down and backwards. This unique and unorthodox style necessitated that the melody be played with the thumb. Accordingly, the bass lines received the bulk of the attention from her fingers, creating Libba's signature sound that is difficult for even an adept right-handed player to replicate.

Mike Seeger pointed me in the direction of Larry Ellis Sr., one of Libba's several grown grandchildren who was the legal executor of her estate. We exchanged several cordial and productive phone conversations and eventually agreed on basic specifications that didn't stray too far from the Steve Howe model. We did enhance the 12th-fret inlay with a stylized mother-of-pearl Freight Train. Elizabeth Cotten's modest signature graced the space between the 19th and 20th frets, and Larry Ellis Sr. co-signed the interior edition labels with Chris Martin.

Prior to the instrument's unveiling at the Anaheim NAMM Show in January of 2001, I received a call from Libba's great grandson John Evans, a computer consultant from Charlotte, North Carolina. His young son Jordan was very interested in the guitar and being left-handed, he was learning to play in the style of his great great grandmother. With the help of Mike Seeger, we arranged for Jordan to receive one of the commemorative edition guitars, laying the groundwork for Jordan to continue his family's legacy.

Opposite page: The Elizabeth Cotten 00-18CTN Commemorative Edition complete with mother-of-pearl freight train at the octave fret. Left: 'Libba' Cotten with her original Martin 00-18. Right: The classic 00 14-fret design is reincarnated in 2003 as a Vintage Series 00-18V.

00-18V

More than a year after working on the Elizabeth Cotten Signature Edition, I found myself at Catherine Jacobs' and Fred Oster's Vintage Instrument Shop in Philadelphia with fellow Martin dealer Richard Johnston of Gryphon Stringed Instruments and legendary guitarist Martin Carthy. Martin and I were finalizing the specifications for his 000-18MC signature edition, but the conversation strayed down a size to the 00-18.

The unanimous complaint was that there simply weren't enough of these instruments to satisfy the demand. In particular, the comfortable Grand Concert shape lends itself perfectly to women and smaller players. Everyone agreed that it was high time to reinstate the 00-18 to its rightful place among the stock Martin offerings. I took this suggestion very seriously and carried the message loud and clear back to the factory with the hope that a faithful 00-18V would be prototyped and introduced. You'll have to check a current Martin price list to see whether this initiative came to fruition. If it has, thank Steve Howe, Elizabeth Cotten, Bob Dylan, and the participants of that passionate conversation.

In the words of John Ullman, who together with his partner, Irene Namkung, co-managed Elizabeth Cotten's career from 1974 to 1987: "If Libba Cotten were to be described by just one word, it would be indomitable. Beneath her kindly grandmother exterior was immense personal strength and a powerful sense of purpose. From the sixties until just before her death in 1987, she toured tirelessly. Always the audiences came to hear Libba's music and left inspired by her spirit. Her stories were often funny, but implied the strength she mustered to transcend the hardships of poverty, racism, and age."

The 00-18CTN commemorates that indomitable spirit and passes it on through music to future generations.

Elizabeth Cotten was faithful to the 00-18 that she used in performances and recordings throughout the full span of her professional career.

PHILADELPHIA FOLK FESTIVAL
40TH ANNIVERSARY MPFF EDITION
Intricate inlay and fine materials honor the premier folk festival

THE PHILADELPHIA FOLK FESTIVAL, held every summer in Schwenksville, Pennsylvania, has evolved from a small, grass-roots event into a three-day family-oriented celebration attracting folk music enthusiasts from around the globe. The festival features an amazing list of performers, folk and square dancing, workshops, arts and crafts, and camping.

The acoustic guitar is key to virtually all the music performed at the festival, and Martin has always played an important role as collaborator, supporter and sponsor of the festival. The very first Philadelphia Folk Festival was considered something of a financial risk to the organizers and Frank Martin, president of Martin at the time, eased the pressure by guaranteeing to make up a limited amount of losses should they have occurred. Though the funds were never needed, Martin's commitment to the festival was important and has been carried on through the years.

In the early eighties, I was managing The 1833 Shop and attending festivals with the Custom Shop van was a key part of my job. One hot afternoon at the Martin booth, I met a lovely woman named Susan Ellis and I ended up marrying her. And so the Festival is, for obvious reasons, very special to me.

An evolving array of Martin employees volunteered annually to set up a display of instruments in the crafts area so that festival-goers could try an assortment of models. Martin also provided a guitar for the festival raffle that was invariably a tremendous success. The raffle provided a significant fundraising vehicle for the Folksong Society and it was a very effective promotional tool for Martin. The Folkfest raffle procedure provided a successful template for dozens of other music festivals across the country.

In 2001, Martin sponsored the festival's much needed new main stage. Part of that sponsorship discussion involved the idea of creating a Philadelphia Folk Festival 40th Anniversary Edition guitar. The "M" model, a thin-bodied stage and studio guitar inspired by the Martin's 1930s arch-tops, was a logical starting point. David Bromberg had offered his expertise in assessing the M-model prototypes at their inception in the late seventies. The resulting Grand Auditorium guitars enjoyed popularity from folk musicians for their balance and recordability. David Bromberg in particular liked the fact that the notes would resonate and decay quickly (making room for new notes) without the thicker resonant overtones typically produced by larger rosewood Dreadnoughts.

Constructed with East Indian rosewood back and sides, the MPFF utilizes an Engelmann spruce soundboard with scalloped X-braces. The headstock is adorned with the exquisite modified torch inlay, a pattern that first appeared in 1902 but was abandoned in favor of the simplified "torch" or "flowerpot" headplate. The festival's distinctive banjo logo is inlaid in mother of pearl at the 5th fret and "Philadelphia Folk Festival" in stylized lettering graces the end of the fingerboard. The very first prototype, featuring handcut inlays by David Nichols of Custom Pearl Inlay Co. in Malone, New York, was raffled to a lucky winner at the 2001 festival, preceding the model's introduction at the Anaheim NAMM Show in January of 2002.

Above: The MPFF model was inspired by the Grand Auditorium M-38, a guitar embraced by the folk-music community because of its tonal balance both on stage and in the studio. Left: The main "Martin Stage" at the 2001 "40th Anniversary" of the Philadelphia Folk Festival. Appropriately, David Bromberg is on stage with his Martin M-model.

ARLO GUTHRIE 0000-28HAG

Tales from a great guitar family

ARLO GUTHRIE, SON OF LEGENDARY FOLK SINGER and songwriter Woody Guthrie, learned to play guitar by the age of six. Although his father was hospitalized for many of his early years, Arlo grew up with the likes of Pete Seeger, Bob Dylan, and Leadbelly. By the time he was in his teens Arlo was performing in coffee houses. His epic song "Alice's Restaurant," the classic anti-Establishment folk song, helped define the Woodstock era. The true events surrounding a pile of garbage and Arlo's escapades with the police and the draft board actually occurred in October of 1965. The album *Alice's Restaurant*, released two years later in October of 1967, launched Arlo to the forefront of the antiwar movement in the late sixties and early seventies.

As an active touring artist, Arlo had plenty of reason to stay in relatively constant touch with the Martin Guitar Company. He was a tried-and-true owner of an M-38, his primary performance guitar, and the Guthrie household certainly contained many other Martin

Arlo performs at the Philadelphia Folk Festival with his array of 6-string and 12-string M-sized Martins.

His epic song "Alice's Restaurant," the classic anti-Establishment folk song, helped define the Woodstock era.

Opposite Page: Detail of the Arlo Guthrie 000012-28HAG Signature Edition 12-string, complete with circles and arrows and a paragraph on the back of each one! Left: The old church that housed Alice's Restaurant is captured on an engraved pearl headstock inlay. Right: Arlo's companion 6-string 0000-28HAG Edition.

instruments. One was a 00-17 that Woody Guthrie had presented to Arlo as a child. Another was the substantially modified D-18, complete with Yin/Yang symbol in the headstock that Arlo had performed with at Woodstock. And with her 00-15 Martin, Arlo's daughter Sarah Lee was carrying on the family tradition as a solo performer, a collaborator with her husband Johnny Irion, and a member of her father's band. So Arlo was in touch with Martin often, his phone calls and visits always interesting and invariably humorous.

During one such conversation, Arlo revealed to me that 1997 was officially the thirtieth anniversary of the *Alice's Restaurant* recording. As one who had committed the entire Massacre lyric to memory, I felt that this in itself was deserving of a Signature Edition. We got right to work. In order to capture the flavor of the song, some special inlays were in order. Within the lyrics, Arlo continually reminds the listener about the many items that were collected as evidence against him and marked by Officer Obie with "circles and arrows and a paragraph on the back of each one."

Larry Sifel and Jeff Harding of Pearlworks executed a stunning abalone-bordered mother-of-pearl engraved oval depicting Alice's Restaurant, the notorious church building in Stockbridge, Massachusetts where the infamous "Massacre" occurred. Being great Arlo fans themselves, Larry Sifel and Jeff Harding of Pearlworks also volunteered the clever motif of circles and arrows for the fingerboards of the matching 6- and 12-string editions. We built four prototypes, two of each model, with surprisingly successful results. A special blue-jean covered hardshell case was created to house each of the guitars.

Arlo was touring with post-Jerry Garcia remnants of the Grateful Dead under the moniker of The Further Festival. I met him, prototypes in hand, at the outdoor Montage Mountain venue in the Poconos. Arlo greeted me in the backstage cafeteria, where we were soon joined by Mickey Hart, Bob Weir, and Hot Tuna/Jefferson Airplane guitarist Jorma Kaukonen. After an intense half-hour jam, Jorma scrutinized the fingerboard with a puzzled look and asked: "What are these?"

I replied: "Those are Officer Obie's circles and arrows."

He scratched his head and said: "Yea, but where's the paragraph on the back of each one?" Everyone laughed at Jorma's idea. I grabbed a sheet of paper and the three of us wrote a perfectly pertinent paragraph. There was a spot "on the back" of each guitar, visible through the soundhole. A second interior label would provide the ideal panel for our freshly conceived paragraph.

In commemoration of the thirtieth anniversary of the legendary recording, the edition was limited to just thirty of each model. The charitable proceeds were donated to Arlo's Interfaith Church Foundation, which is housed in the same church where he wrote *Alice's Restaurant* and where the movie of the same name was filmed in 1969.

JUDY COLLINS HD-35SJC/HD12-35SJC

Suite, soothing, and graceful

WHEN THE BRAND NEW Sycamore Street factory opened in 1964, Martin management wanted to make a big splash. An open house was held and two of the key talents in the New York folk community were lured out to Nazareth to perform on the back loading dock for the employees and townsfolk. For their remuneration, Judy Collins and Tom Paxton each received a custom-made pearl-rosetted herringbone custom-made D-28. Reports would indicate that the afternoon was unforgettable.

Each in their own way, these gifted performers have left their indelible mark on American culture. Tom Paxton expressed tremendous integrity with his pen, voice, and guitar, unleashing a barrage of topical songs with poetic depth and political wit. Judy on the other hand found her voice in the traditional songs of the folk revival. Abandoning a promising career as a classical pianist, she donned an acoustic guitar and started singing in folk clubs. Inspired by many of the young songwriters of Greenwich Village, Judy was one of the first to introduce the songs of Bob Dylan, Phil Ochs, Joni Mitchell, Leonard Cohen, and Randy Newman to the American public. In many cases, she served as the catalyst for their careers.

From the mid sixties into the early seventies, Judy embraced a broader musical palette well outside the folk genre with hit singles like "Both Sides Now," "Chelsea Morning," and "Send In The Clowns." For the new millennium, she established her own record label, Wildflower Records. After a lifetime on stage, she still performs frequently. Her satin voice, warmth, and ease onstage keep the seats at all her shows filled.

Lee Walesyn, a retired Pennsylvania State Policeman and avid Martin guitar collector, had attended one of Judy's concerts up in Nantucket. She autographed her page in Lee's copy of the Washburn/Johnston Martin book. Several days later, Lee visited the Martin factory and stopped by my office. "I don't mean to bother you, but you know you really should do a Judy Collins Signature Edition."

There was no question that he was right. I had furnished Judy with a guitar case several months back and had an email address. That afternoon I sent her a brief message expressing interest in a collaboration. It didn't take long for Judy to email me her typically warm and personal response. As luck would have it, she was on tour for the Christmas holidays and was scheduled to perform at the nearby State Theater in Easton, PA. I immediately made arrangements to meet her at soundcheck. I found her full of energy and magnetism.

Judy has owned and performed with quite an assortment of Martin guitars throughout her career. Her most prized instrument had long been her Martin D12-35 12-fret 12-string that she loves for vocal accompaniment. We discussed a few ideas about replicating it. I immediately thought of the Dave Matthews' model with its three-piece back of rosewood and padauk. I explained the elegance of using a contrasting center wedge to Judy and she loved the idea. We decided on the spot that the wedge should be flamed maple.

As show time drew near, Judy asked whether I had family. I showed her a photo of my young daughters Emily and Grace, who were two and six respectively at the time. She urged me to call them and have them come down for the concert. My wife dressed the girls in their crimson Christmas dresses and before we knew it we were seated directly in front of the microphone on the first row. The children were spellbound. Early in the show, Judy knelt down and sang Silver Bells directly to them. We'll never forget that!

After the holidays, I worked on the specifications and inlay designs for Judy's model. We exchanged many emails and decided it would be advantageous to meet up again.

I had been both a student and a teacher at the small private school of Blair Academy in Blairstown, New Jersey. Blair had booked Judy for their holiday concert and fundraiser so I drove up for the show to meet Judy and her husband Louis Nelson. Louis and I looked over the numerous guitar design laserprint options that I had brought for the purposes of discussion. I had suggested that we offer both matching 6- and 12-string models, given that the market for 12-strings is more limited. We took our time with the prototypes. The inlays were time consuming enough, and the finishing department was quite challenged with keeping the dark filler off of the white maple. Two years had passed since our first meeting at The State Theater. Once again, Christmas was fast approaching and Judy was once more spreading the joy of the season, this time in the nearby town of Wilkes Barre. It was my distinct pleasure to deliver one of each of the two matching prototypes to Judy backstage prior to the show. She loved the guitars and played them on stage that night, and for many nights to come.

Fifty of the HD-35SJC 6-string guitars and thirty-three of the HD12-35SJC 12-string models were made. In accordance with Judy's wishes, the charitable proceeds from the project were split evenly between the United Nations Children's Fund (UNICEF) and Amnesty International.

Left: Judy Collins' HD12-35SJC 12-String Signature Edition is graced with Judy's signature and her record-company logo, a delicate wildflower, inlaid in mother-of-pearl and abalone into a black ebony headplate. Right: The center wedge of the three-piece back is cut from flamed maple to contrast with dark wings of East Indian rosewood.

ROGER MCGUINN
D12-42RM
A folk legend inspires an optimum 12-string Dreadnought edition

DAN VANDERHAAR IS A VERY DEDICATED Martin enthusiast. In addition to his passion for our instruments, he's very good at finding things, in particular, anything remotely associated with Martin guitars. Many years back, he started sending us an occasional album cover or poster. When we were looking to add greater scope and interest to our lobby display, we gave him the latitude to pull together a more comprehensive collection of significant album covers, CDs, and photographs of famous artists with their Martin guitars. He did a great job. Our ever-expanding "Wall Of Fame" is living proof.

Dan is also a collector of autographs and occasionally he would drop me an email about a particular artist that he had seen in concert. Being a huge Byrds fan, he was very excited about having met and talked to Roger McGuinn. An excited email message from Dan reminded me what a great candidate Roger would be for a signature edition. Of course, Dan supplied me with Roger's email address, so I followed Dan's lead.

Roger was touring a circuit of interesting larger clubs. I noticed that he was scheduled to play "At The Tabernacle" in Mt. Tabor, New Jersey, a unique and historical circular auditorium that was booking some pretty high-end folk acts. I called my roommate from college and made arrangements to meet him there. For extra ammunition, I took a few special guitars including my custom "Vine Of Harmonics" 12-string.

I met Roger and his wife Camilla backstage. They were both outgoing and warm. Roger was excited about a signature model and it didn't take us long to identify a direction to take. He wanted a 14-fret Dreadnought 12-string pearled up with Style-42 appointments. He had a 12-fret D12-35 that he had used as his primary acoustic guitar with the Byrds, but he found the string-changing process on a slotted head to be tedious, so for the D12-42RM we opted for a solid headstock. Easy action is the key to a great 12-string and we took particular care in making sure the McGuinn model was specified low and buttery. We added Roger's signature at the last fret and in classic McGuinn style, we created a hardshell vintage Geib-style case with a black denim exterior.

The prototypes were superb. We went to the trade show fully aware that the market for high-end 12-strings was limited, but clearly these guitars represented the most striking and playable 12-strings that Martin had ever offered.

The best aspect of the project was Roger's enthusiasm. In addition to number one of the edition, he ordered several extras and fully embraced his signature model as his preference on tour. His love of these acoustic guitars also brought him back to the 6-string guitar, specifically an HD-28V model that reminded him of later Byrds days with bandmate Clarence White.

For me, the highest degree of satisfaction comes from providing exceptional tools to inspired musicians from whom great music can be realized.

Top: The Roger McGuinn D12-42RM Signature Edition with its special black-denim Geib-style case. Bottom: The combination of a solid headstock for ease of stringing, elegant Style-42 pearl, and onboard electronics, yielded one of the finest Martin 12-string models ever offered.

CLARENCE WHITE D-18CW/D-28CW/D-28CWB
Legacies, lightning licks, and large soundholes

I FIRST HEARD TONY RICE PERFORM as a member of David Grisman's band at the Guild Of American Luthier's Convention held in San Francisco in the early eighties. I remember being confused about the guitar he was playing, especially since I prided myself on being able to quickly identify Martin models. The body appeared to be that of a D-28, but the soundhole was much too large, and the fingerboard, extending partway into the soundhole, was bound like a D-35. The tone of this unique guitar was hollow and powerful in Tony's hands. I soon learned that it was a D-28 made in 1935 and that it had belonged to the highly revered flatpicking guitarist Clarence White. Legend had it that Clarence was a bit heavy handed with his pick, and that the lip of the soundhole had been badly worn away. Another less glamorous story suggested that Clarence used to put out his cigarette butts on the lip of the soundhole. In any event, somewhere during its colorful history the instrument was taken into a guitar repair shop and the diameter of the soundhole was expanded to a point just inside the first rosette rings. In addition, the badly worn fingerboard was replaced with an ebony Gretsch board, bound in white and longer than a Martin board.

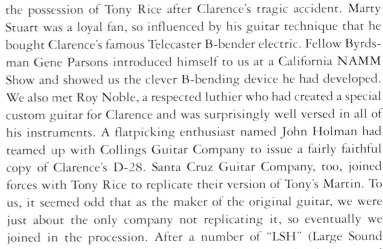

To the average person, Clarence White is obscure, but in guitar circles he is certainly legendary. While still in his teens, Clarence developed a playing style of lightning runs, syncopated picking, and sophisticated rhythms that transformed bluegrass guitar into a lead instrument for the first time. The Kentucky Colonels, founded with his brother Roland in 1961, showcased Clarence's dazzling technique on several albums, but it wasn't until he joined forces with Roger McGuinn and the Byrds that he received national acclaim. He played on six Byrds albums and innumerable live shows until the group disbanded in 1973.

A band with fellow bluegrassers David Grisman, Peter Rowan, Richard Greene, and Bill Keith for a televised concert became Muleskinner, whose album, *A Potpourri Of Bluegrass Jam*, marked the beginning of jazz-inspired progressive bluegrass.

Following Muleskinner, Clarence reunited with his brothers Roland and Eric to form the New Kentucky Colonels, but it was to be brief. On July 14, 1973, he was struck and killed by a drunk driver while loading equipment after a show in Palmdale, California. He left behind a legacy of great playing that continues to influence and challenge flatpickers worldwide.

At Martin, we learned about Clarence through a number of different channels. We knew that the unusual guitar had come into the possession of Tony Rice after Clarence's tragic accident. Marty Stuart was a loyal fan, so influenced by his guitar technique that he bought Clarence's famous Telecaster B-bender electric. Fellow Byrdsman Gene Parsons introduced himself to us at a California NAMM Show and showed us the clever B-bending device he had developed. We also met Roy Noble, a respected luthier who had created a special custom guitar for Clarence and was surprisingly well versed in all of his instruments. A flatpicking enthusiast named John Holman had teamed up with Collings Guitar Company to issue a fairly faithful copy of Clarence's D-28. Santa Cruz Guitar Company, too, joined forces with Tony Rice to replicate their version of Tony's Martin. To us, it seemed odd that as the maker of the original guitar, we were just about the only company not replicating it, so eventually we joined in the procession. After a number of "LSH" (Large Sound Hole) limited editions and a Vintage Series "LSH" Herringbone 28, we were finally put in touch with Clarence's daughter Michelle White Bledsoe. She was in control of her father's estate and was excited about the prospect of finally working with Martin on the licensing of a model to commemorate her father's incredible contribution to guitar music.

Reluctant to be perceived as copying the competition, we focused first on Clarence's "other" Martin — his 1952 D-18 that he preferred for lead picking in the sixties. Primarily through the efforts of Martin clinician and bluegrass virtuoso Richard Starkey, we developed specifications for a 2001 Limited Edition offering that blended quilted mahogany for the back and sides with rare Appalachian spruce for the soundboard. The resulting D-18CW Clarence White Commemorative Edition guitars were tonally extraordinary and instantly successful, selling a total of 292 special instruments.

In 2002, after the D-18CW guitars had all been assimilated into the marketplace, we iced the cake by unveiling our own Limited Edition Brazilian rosewood and East Indian rosewood versions of the original Clarence White D-28, complete with Adirondack tops, enlarged soundholes, and bound fingerboards. The D-28CWB and D-28CW Clarence White Commemorative Editions blended premium tonewoods, Golden Era® construction, and the original guitar's unique appointments. The resulting instruments captured the clarity, power and balanced timbre that Clarence White found advantageous in his Martin guitars. Some twenty-five years after his passing, his brilliance with a flatpick continues to awe, influence, and motivate a new generation of guitar players.

The distinctive bound fingerboard, tortoise-colored pickguard, and long-saddled bridge of the Clarence White D-28CW Commemorative Edition.

69

DAVID CROSBY
D-18DC

Wooden ships on the water

I FIRST MET DAVID CROSBY BACKSTAGE at the Telluride Bluegrass Festival while delivering the D-42JC prototype to Johnny Cash. It was a very quick introduction. I followed him hurriedly down the path, told him who I was and that I hoped to continue the conversation at a less harried time. Following that initial introduction, we worked with some of David's associates for more than a year to develop a signature edition. When my repeated phone calls remained unanswered, I began to worry that our project was finished. Then, seemingly out of nowhere, I received an email from David. He needed a replacement guitar case.

He was unaware and apologetic that so much had transpired without his knowledge. There had been some problems that had obviously impacted and jeopardized our project, but now we were in direct contact and we were making progress.

David's love of boats prompted several different nautical motifs for the fingerboard and headstock, the final approved version being a simple schooner in mother-of-pearl that nested neatly under the Martin decal logo. From his time with the Byrds to the founding of Crosby, Stills and Nash, David had always been enamored with Martin D-18 models. We decided to create a fairly straightforward Style-18 Dreadnought with enhancements that included an Engelmann spruce soundboard with blue Paua shell rosette, an ebony fingerboard, bridge and headplate, plus tortoise-colored bindings. But by far the most striking aspect of the guitar was the use of rare quilted mahogany for the back and sides. We had acquired enough of this special tonewood to make only a few hundred guitars and it seemed appropriate to earmark it for the Crosby edition. This meant establishing an edition limit of 250 instruments.

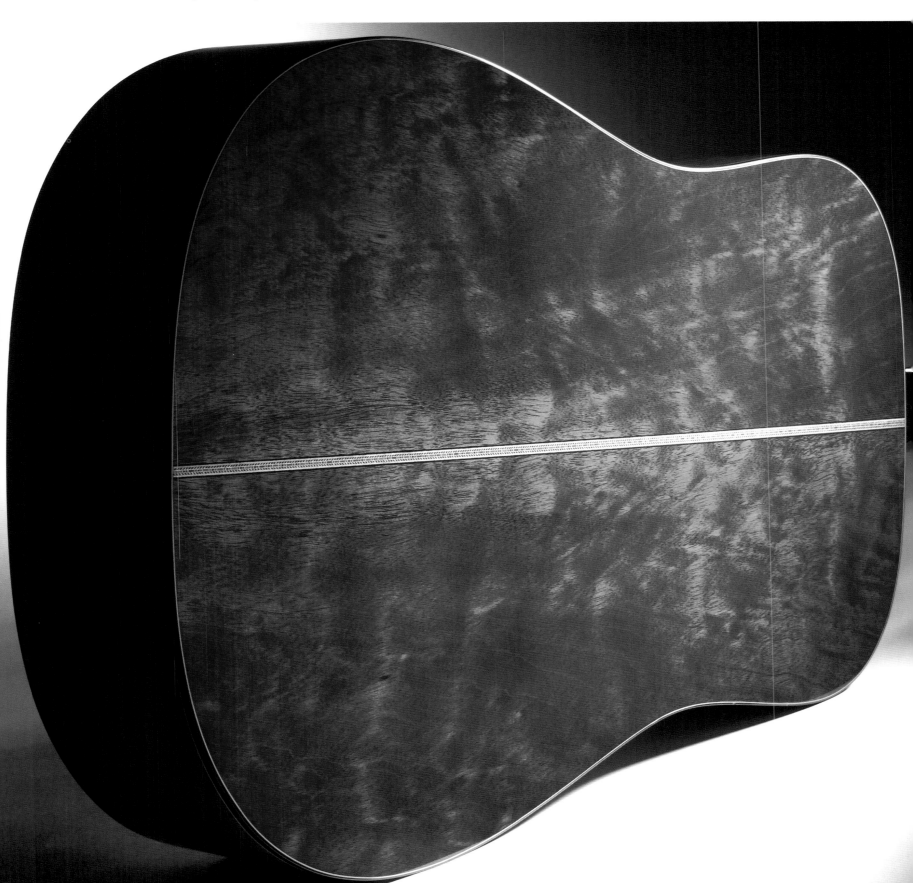

It is always special when an artist truly loves the instrument and David certainly did. He retired the Martin D-45 that he had been using for years in favor of the new signature edition.

Our excitement about David's edition grew as the prototypes neared completion. We were especially surprised at what a tremendous impact the Engelmann spruce top had upon the tonal dynamics of the guitar. Beyond that, the instrument was beautiful in its simplicity and taste.

The week that I took David's prototype out to shipping was also the week that my cardiologist informed me that I would be needing a bypass operation. This meant that I would miss the show. I was disappointed, but two days before my surgery an ecstatic David Crosby called, prototype in hand.

It is always a special occasion when an artist calls to acknowledge receipt of a guitar. It is even more special when they truly love the instrument and David certainly did. Contractually, he had the right to order a number of instruments from the edition and nearly everyone in David's closer circle wanted to be included. Most significantly, he retired the Martin D-45 that he had been using for years in favor of the new signature edition.

Crosby, Stills, Nash and Young were scheduled to play Philadelphia on their tour in early 2002. I attended with my associate Chris Thomas. Just prior to the start of the show, we caught up with Stephen Stills' (and Paul Simon's) guitar tech Michael Kaye who was kind enough invite us to the show in the first place. We had the opportunity to meet Alan Rogan, a veteran guitar technician who had worked with everyone from George Harrison to The Who. Alan was tending to Graham Nash's guitars throughout the tour and during our conversation, Graham stopped by to say hello. I had heard a great deal about Graham's love of art and photography and we had a nice conversation about M.C. Escher, graphic art and black-and-white photography.

Of course, I alluded to the fact that he was next in line for an edition and after I returned to Nazareth, I sent a small collection of my pen-and-ink prints along with a follow-up note about a Graham Nash Signature Edition and sure enough, before the month was out, we were on the phone talking specifications.

Left: The rare and beautiful grain patterning of quilted mahogany graces the back of the Clarence White D-18CW (previous page) as well as David Crosby's D-18DC Signature Edition. Above: David performs at the Telluride Bluegrass Festival with his Martin D-45. Right: A delicate pearl schooner is nested beneath the Martin logo on the D-18DC headplate.

STEPHEN STILLS D-45SS
A loyal enthusiast, an expert collector, and a legendary player

N AUGUST OF 1995 I RECEIVED A CALL from Martin's California District Sales Manager Dan Gulino concerning Stephen Stills. Dan had become friends with Tom Lowrey, Stephen's guitar technician and assistant at that time. Tom suggested that Stephen might be interested in a signature-model collaboration — we were certainly interested in Stephen. From our perspective, the whole Crosby, Stills, Nash and Young band was immensely significant, but we had to start somewhere.

Very early on in our discussions it became clear that doing a CSN&Y model was going to be a real challenge. It would mean negotiating with an assortment of managers and agents, and it just began to look like a licensing nightmare. So the conversations focused logically on Stephen — after all, he is the most fervent Martin aficionado in the group, a serious Martin collector, and incredibly astute in his knowledge of Martin history and instruments.

Initially, Stephen looked toward the herringbone D-28 as the basis for his signature edition. Actual detailed specifications were developed for an HD-40SS model, but gradually Stephen's love of higher-end vintage models persuaded him in the direction of a Brazilian D-45. He was so excited about the project that he booked a flight just to visit the factory, arriving with a yellow notepad in hand, upon which he had enumerated a lengthy list of details relating to the model. He knew what he was talking about and by the end of the day he had enjoyed an in-depth factory tour and had carefully stipulated all the specifications for a Stephen Stills "Southern Cross" D-45SS Signature Edition of just ninety-one special instruments.

Stephen also fell in love with a Jimmie Rodgers 000-45JR Signature Model along the tour route and, for his daughter, a 00-16DB Women and Music model had caught his eye. We arranged to ship these instruments out to California and began to initiate the prototypes for Stephen's model.

In researching the Southern Cross constellation on the internet, I found the Australian flag and quickly digitized the star configuration for mother-of-pearl inlay into Stephen's pickguards. After a significant amount of labor, Pearlworks sent the first samples, one of which I forwarded to Stephen with great anticipation — only to be informed that there were in fact five stars in the Southern Cross constellation, not six as the flag represented. In spite of this, the error was easy to correct and the prototypes gradually reached completion. We shipped one to Stephen for his comments and he had many: the top was too white and needed toner, one of the bindings was too tall to be indicative of thirties styling, and he wanted the model to be offered with hexagon inlays as well as Style-45 snowflakes (as were the original ninety-one D-45s of the prewar era). Though we were frustrated at not getting everything right on the first pass, it

certainly was a testament to Stephen's great knowledge of our instruments. His fastidious input insured that the model possessed accuracy and integrity.

The edition was unveiled at the Nashville NAMM Show in July of 1998. Stephen attended the show and signed a great deal of autographs, after which we took him out to a great dinner at Morton's to thank him for making the trip to Nashville. The details of that memorable dinner are reserved for another book.

A great deal of support was lent by Stephen's staff: his patient and approachable manager Gerry Tolman, his delightful business manager Kelly Muchoney, and of course Tom Lowrey who got the whole project rolling. We came away from Nashville pretty elated with about half of the edition sold — not bad given that the retail price of the Stills model was $19,000. Stephen had earmarked the Tides Center Foundation as the recipient of the charitable contribution from the project. Those royalties would go a long way in bringing music education to children.

Several weeks after getting back to Nazareth, we received a call from Jacques Grenier, a producer (at that time) for Ted Koppel's *Nightline* show. ABC was looking

> *He was so excited about the project that he booked a flight just to visit the factory.*

to expand their Friday night programming with stories that represented greater human interest and, specifically, they wanted to do a celebrity feature about Martin artists' signature-model projects. We suggested Stephen Stills and Jacques loved the idea.

Stephen returned to Nazareth again to be filmed overseeing the production of his model. Weeks later, ABC reciprocated by flying out to Los Angeles to film Stephen at home with his collection and also in the recording studio with Graham Nash and David Crosby. To cap it off, *Nightline* came to the NAMM Show to interview random customers about Stephen's model. When the edited show aired a month and a half later, the phones rang off the hook and the remaining half of the edition sold out within a day of the airing of the show.

Stephen had ordered several edition guitars for bandmates. One for Neil Young had a customized pickguard with an abalone inlaid broken arrow. Stephen customized his own prototype with his name in large pearl script lettering in the fingerboard. It is certain that Stephen's signature models caught the attention of David Crosby, himself a longtime D-45 owner.

Above: Stephen Stills is as serious about collecting Martin guitars as he is about playing them. Here he is pictured with one of his pre-World War II D-45s, the guitar that provided the basis for his signature edition. Right: Detail of the first prototype of the Stills D-45SS, complete with "Southern Cross" pickguard and like white untoned top.

GRAHAM NASH
000-40Q2GN
Quilted mahogany top to bottom

A NATIVE OF MANCHESTER, England, Graham Nash was among a generation of British youth drawn to the skiffle music popularized by Lonnie Donegan in the fifties. From his early career as a member of the chart-topping Hollies and his thirty-plus year membership with Crosby, Stills, Nash (& Young), to his solo work, songwriting, photography, and social involvement, he has been — and remains — one of rock's most eloquent and respected ambassadors. After joining Crosby, Stills & Nash, Graham's harmony singing and

refined into digital inlay art. A brilliant red composite was chosen for the heart, and the wings were executed in mother-of-pearl against a contrasting black ebony background.

I got carried away in my attempt to contribute inlay designs for the fingerboard. Alluding to Graham's lyrics from "Teach Your Children," I prepared artwork of a "fireplace" inside a very fine "house," with the necessary "two cats in the yard." I faxed these over to Hawaii for Graham. Several days later I called at 6:00 a.m. Hawaii time to find Graham deeply asleep, his wife Susan barely awake. Like a true mainlander, I had miscalculated the time difference, but Susan took it in good stride. I phoned back at a reasonable hour and she calmly explained that my fingerboard ideas weren't going to fly. We settled on a more tasteful Style-42 snowflake pattern with Graham's signature in gold mother-of-pearl between the 17th and 20th frets.

Graham has always been actively involved in charitable concerns. Accordingly, he stipulated that the royalties from the sale of his

Throughout his career, Graham has been — and continues to be — one of rock's most eloquent and respected ambassadors.

writing became integral to the group dynamics. In whichever aggregation, Graham's strong character and genial personality have been key factors in the partnership's longevity.

Alan Rogan took an active roll early on by communicating many of Graham's ideas for a model. Initially, Graham wished to develop several models with varying degrees of ornamentation and pricing. This became rather complicated and we opted to distill these ideas down to a traditional 14-fret 000 with rare and beautiful quilted mahogany on the top, back, and sides.

For the headstock, Graham submitted simple artwork (used by his

signature-edition guitar be donated in support of the Mattel Hospital For Children at UCLA. With his signature edition, Graham joined bandmates Stephen Stills and David Crosby in the select group of musicians honored with signature-edition models. In the view of many, however, Martin remains one guitar short of a full set. Neil Young, are you listening?

Opposite page: The exquisite quilted mahogany top detail of the Graham Nash 000-40Q2GN. Upper left: Graham Nash in action. Upper right: The unusual and rich headstock of the Nash edition features a red coral heart with mother-of-pearl wings against

LIGHTFOOT D-18GL
Not Many But Much

JONI MITCHELL, NEIL YOUNG, K. D. LANG, Bruce Cockburn — Canada has produced some extraordinary singer-songwriters and guitarists, but perhaps no one exemplifies the spirit of Canada and the essence of acoustic music the way that Gordon Lightfoot does. Beginning with his first album in 1966, he quickly developed into a major artist, writing and recording several hit singles, among them classics like "Early Morning Rain," "Beautiful," "If You Could Read My Mind," "Sundown," "Rainy Day People," and "The Wreck Of The Edmund Fitzgerald."

At Martin, we were certainly aware of Gordon. Though he gravitated toward an old Gibson 12-string for several of his songs, Gordon had been playing 6-string Martin Dreadnoughts throughout his entire career, with Martin guitars featured on many of his album covers. It was an innocent call from Gordon's manager Barry Harvey at Early Morning Productions that started our conversations. Barry was very down to earth, affable, and receptive to discussing the notion of a Gordon Lightfoot Signature Edition. It certainly helped that Barry had an abiding respect and knowledge of Martin guitars.

Several weeks passed before Barry called back and affirmed Gordon's desire to pursue a signature model. We exchanged some phone numbers and before long, Gordon was mulling over an assortment of guitar sizes and shapes, tone woods, and relevant charities. Though he owned a D-28, a D-35, and an old 12-fret 000-45, he clearly loved his 1948 D-18 (Serial #105249). Like most Martin D-18s from that era, his guitar was dry, loud, and projective with tremendous brilliance and clarity. The D-18 had always served him well on stage and in the studio and it wasn't long before we focused our design efforts on a traditional vintage D-18 enhanced with the addition of premium tonewoods and classic Martin style.

Engelmann spruce grows high up into the Canadian Rockies. We thought it would be a great choice for the soundboard, especially given its open breathy tone. For the back and sides, we were fortunate to have acquired a relatively small batch of quilted mahogany with its bookmatched mottled grain swirls. The Lightfoot edition would be the first of many signature editions crafted with this rare and beautiful tonewood. Kluson-style tuning machines were selected to match Gordon's original guitar, and an abalone pearl rosette added a fitting splendor to what otherwise were tastefully understated appointments.

To mark the 12th fret, we created a silhouetted profile of the renowned but tragic *Edmund Fitzgerald* freighter with a shimmering watery reflection in several shades of pearl against the black ebony sky, and Gordon Lightfoot's signature graced the final two frets.

Appropriately, the charitable proceeds from the sale of the D-18GL guitars were donated in support of the Gordon Lightfoot Scholarship Fund at Great Lakes Maritime Academy (part of Northwestern Michigan College), home to the only officer training program for freshwater maritime ships in the United States. Gordon established the fund in 1976 to help prevent shipping disasters like the sinking of the *Edmund Fitzgerald*, which inspired perhaps his most memorable song.

The Nashville NAMM Show is a much smaller trade show than the one held in Anaheim. Accordingly, the limited editions introduced in Nashville were often smaller in edition size and targeted to more specific markets. Frankly, I didn't have a sense for how well a Gordon Lightfoot model would be received. When I asked Gordon whether any particular number appealed to him, he mentioned sixty-one — his age at the time. I liked the sound of the number as well. "Highway 61" was a significant Dylan tune and I suspected that Gordon had traversed that route many times over during his colorful career. So sixty-one it was!

Like most Martin D-18s from that era, his guitar was dry, loud, and projective with tremendous brilliance and clarity.

What I didn't anticipate was an instantaneous sellout of the edition. Martin dealers and district sales managers alike were all upset with me for what in hindsight was obviously an inadequate edition quantity. As a result, future editions would generally be offered with a specified ordering period instead of a predetermined fixed quantity. Nevertheless, the Gordon Lightfoot signature guitars are marked with a particular integrity — just like the man who inspired them — and their scarcity makes them all the more special.

The Gordon Lightfoot Signature Edition D-18GL was limited to just sixty-one guitars. In hindsight it appears that there were hundreds more wanting these special instruments.

DAN FOGELBERG
D-41DF
Integrity, taste and detail

STEPHEN STILLS' FORMER GUITAR TECHNICIAN Tom Lowrey was helpful through the years in helping Martin identify loyal Martin players. In one of our many conversations, Tom mentioned that he had had a conversation with Dan Fogelberg, that Dan was a real Martin fan, and that he would be a worthy of consideration for a limited-edition guitar collaboration. We agreed!

In the fall of 2000 we took notice that Dan was scheduled to perform locally at the beautifully renovated State Theater in nearby Easton, PA. Dan was represented by Nina Avermides of HK Management — who managed Jimmy Buffett — and because of our successful project with Jimmy, it was perfectly appropriate to contact Nina to see whether Dan would have any interest in visiting the factory while he was in the area. She quickly got word to Dan of our interest in him and he responded with great enthusiasm. We arranged to meet at the State Theater during the usual late-afternoon soundcheck. When he finished we went backstage to his dressing room and talked about our mutual affinity for Martin guitars. He unpacked his weathered D-41 carefully from its case for my inspection: gold Grover Rotomatic tuners, East Indian rosewood back and sides, abalone hexagon inlays, a round and full neck, a nicely aged Sitka spruce top, polished gloss lacquer, and the big deep sound so typical of Martin Dreadnoughts. It wasn't his only Martin but it had been his primary workhorse for songwriting, recording, and performing for nearly three decades.

That evening's concert was completely sold out. After all, Dan had built his career on the expression of his generation's most intimate thoughts and feelings in words and melodies both simple and eloquent. Inspired by success and a new home in the mountains of Colorado, Fogelberg wrote and recorded several of his finest works throughout the seventies and eighties. His unswerving dedication to his craft has earned him some of the most loyal fans in the business and they were out in good numbers that evening at the State Theater.

Early the next morning, Dan arrived at Martin looking refreshed. We took him on a brief tour then sat down to hash out the details of a signature model. Given his love of nature and his concern for the environment, the theme of the guitar quickly took shape.

Dan asked that we develop a snowcapped Colorado mountain motif for the headstock, for which we created some beautiful designs, but he eventually reverted to a slight alteration of the traditional D-41 headplate from "C. F. Martin" to "D. F. Martin." The idea didn't fly with Martin's trademark attorney, though, who simply didn't wish to weaken the brand by establishing any confusing precedents.

Dan's expressive signature graced the final fret of the fingerboard and Colorado was represented with unique mother-of-pearl winter snowflakes in the wings of the bridge. To add a touch of vintage integrity, grained ivoroid was specified for all the bindings, otherwise the guitar was a faithful recreation of Dan's original D-41, down to the original's abalone hexagons beginning at the 3rd fret.

We offered 141 of these beautiful D-41s, each bearing an interior label signed by Dan Fogelberg and Chris Martin. At Dan's request, the charitable proceeds from each guitar were donated to the World Wildlife Fund, the most significant privately funded conservation organization in the world. As with all signature-edition projects, the most exciting moment is when the prototype guitar is delivered to the artist. Upon receipt, Dan answered us with this heartfelt email:

I have just recieved the prototype signature D-41DF and am completely blown away. You people have truly outdone yourselves. I've never heard a better sounding guitar right out of the case. It is so much louder than any of my other 41's or 45's and so beautifully balanced. It's almost scary to think how good it's going to sound in ten or twenty years! The workmanship is stunning, the inlay is spectacular and the choice of woods is exquisite. I'm amazed at the delicacy of the mother-of-pearl snowflakes on the bridge saddle. What a splendid touch.

I couldn't be more delighted with the guitar and so appreciate this prestigious honor by Martin. This instrument will be a cherished and revered friend for the rest of my life. You have once again proven that no one on earth makes finer acoustic guitars than C. F. Martin. Please extend my thanks and congratulations to all the fine folks who contributed to its creation!

Background: Dan Fogelberg with the D-41 that has served as his primary acoustic guitar throughout his career.
Inset: The D-41DF Signature Edition was a straightforward replica of Dan's D-41 with several enhancements, such as the addition of Colorado snowflakes in pearl on the bridge wings.

DON MCLEAN
D-40DM
A generous helping of American Pie

THERE AREN'T MANY MUSICIANS out there that have been as loyal to Martin guitars throughout their careers as Don McLean. He has amassed many over the years: a 00-21, two 000-28s, a 000-45, two D-35S 12-fret models, three D-28s, a D-40 Brazilian Edition, a pair of D-41s, a pair of D-45s, and several customs. He swears by them.

When we first made contact with Don and mentioned the possibility of doing a signature edition, he was extremely flattered; in fact he said that given a choice between a Grammy and the honor of being chosen for a Martin limited edition signature model, he'd "take the Martin any day."

We started conceptualizing the possibilities right away. Don wasn't shy about sharing his favorite features or offering his input

pattern was chosen for the remaining position markers. Upon very close inspection however, an adept observer might determine that the stylized lettering had been routed into a sheet of clear acrylic from the underside, filled with temperature-curing crimson epoxy. The epoxy was then sanded flush with the acrylic and laminated to an extremely thin layer of abalone shell. Each inlay was subsequently trimmed and installed abalone-side down into the ebony fingerboard. The top layer of durable clear acrylic was then contoured to the radius of the fingerboard and polished to a high gloss, serving to protect the playing surface and reflect (literally) the significant words of the song: "King," "Queen," "Jester," "Father," "Son," "Holy Ghost," "Jack Flash," and "American Pie" from an abalone substrate lying underneath the clear acrylic surface. The degree of detail in the inlays was visually dramatic, but the real significance of the process was so subtle that it was most likely overlooked by everyone. This clever technique, developed by Larry Sifel and Jeff Harding of Pearlworks, can potentially reduce the amount of abalone shell required for inlay by more than 80 percent. With the increasing scarcity of abalone, it is likely that this innovative technique will be revisited in the future when supply and yield issues become absolutely critical.

about appointments that would make his model special. We decided to focus on his legendary song "American Pie" as the theme.

Don wanted to be directly involved with the project. He loved the entire process of designing, prototyping, marketing, and finally manufacturing the instruments. During an excursion from his home in Maine to New York City, he diverted west to Nazareth for a brisk February day at the factory to hone the final designs. The guitar was to be a 14-fret Dreadnought with an Engelmann spruce top and East Indian rosewood back and sides. Enhancements included an abalone pearl rosette, forward-shifted scalloped braces, and a modified version of the traditional Martin "torch" inlay pattern.

But by far the most unique idea that Don conceived for his model was the fingerboard with its highly detailed inlay pattern. Like other artist editions, Don McLean's smooth signature was inlaid in mother-of-pearl at the final fret and Martin's standard large hexagon

Small details like this were very important to Don. To match the *American Pie* album-cover artwork, the interior label for each instrument included Don's "thumbs up" logo, complete with a hand-colored American flag and single-star motif. The edition size was limited to no more than seventy-one instruments in keeping with the year the song was written.

It wasn't difficult for Don to choose a charity. He had initiated his own Don McLean Foundation years before in support of homeless shelters, daycare centers, teenage halfway houses, and soup kitchens. Don was especially proud that his foundation had achieved an extremely low overhead which meant that the highest percentage of funds actually made it to the people who needed the assistance.

Above Left: The headstock of the Don McLean Signature Edition combines the Martin decal logo in pearl with the elegant torch inlay pattern. Above Right: Don's attention to detail shows in his signature, interior label art, and unique fingerboard inlay process.

JIM CROCE D-21JC
And you can keep the dime

ONE AFTERNOON, A CALL CAME IN FROM a professional guitar player in southern California named Michael Bizar. He had some questions about Martin guitars, and during our conversation revealed that he was playing and recording with A. J. Croce, the son of the legendary Jim Croce. With some gentle prodding, Michael gave me A. J.'s phone number. I soon called him to propose a special guitar to pay tribute to Jim Croce's incredible musical legacy. A. J. explained that his mother, Jim's widow Ingrid Croce, was the right person with whom to discuss such things.

Having struggled through many difficult years following the tragic plane crash that ended Jim's life in 1973, Ingrid had emerged as a successful restauranteur with her own unique establishment "Croce's," that includes two restaurants, three bars, and great live music nightly in San Diego's historic "Gaslamp District."

Paul and I spent a good bit of time discussing the features that we felt might be appropriate for a Jim Croce commemorative. Because of its grassroots appeal, the D-21 seemed a reasonable choice for a Croce edition. C. F. Martin III loved the 21-Style for its simple elegance. Given that Paul's D-21 was made in 1969, we felt we should offer the model in both Brazilian and East Indian rosewood configurations, since that was the year of the switch from Brazilian to Indian rosewood. We pored through Jim's albums and lyrics to find an appropriate image to work as a fingerboard or headplate inlay. When we came upon Jim's song "Operator," we found the last line "You can keep the dime." I contacted my friend Paul Reitmeir, a coin collector and dealer, who was able to find enough mint condition 1973 dimes to make up both editions of seventy-three guitars each. The dimes were inlaid face up at the 3rd-fret position and encased for their protection in a clear hardened resin.

Martin instruments from the sixties had headstock corners that were rounded to a greater degree than the standard squared design, due to the gradual wear of the fixtures that held the necks during the shaping process. This subtle feature was carefully replicated for the edition, plus close recreations of the original chrome Grover 102C tuning machines were specified. For Jim's love of informality we furnished a black-denim covered hardshell case for each guitar.

Ingrid loved the idea of a Jim Croce edition and we quickly agreed on a plan to initiate a model. When I asked whether she might have any old photos of Jim with Martin guitars, she suggested that I contact Paul Wilson, a photographer in the Philadelphia area who had been a friend and associate of Jim's. Upon contacting Paul, he offered to make the hour drive up to Nazareth to discuss the project. To my surprise, he arrived the next day with an old 1969 Martin D-21 under his arm and a stack of beautiful photographs of Jim from an album-cover photo shoot depicting Jim with the very same D-21 guitar.

Paul explained that while Jim did not record with the D-21, he did occasionally take it on tour. The Martin guitars on Jim's recordings were played by Maury Muehleisne, who owned a D-28 and a D-35. Maury's phrasing was not only an extension of Jim's vocals but was considered by many to be on a virtuoso performance level. Jim did own a 000-28 that he played around the house, primarily for songwriting.

The interior labels for the Jim Croce edition were signed by Ingrid Croce and Chris Martin. A secondary label featured Paul Wilson's color photograph. The charitable proceeds from the sale of each guitar were donated to the "Jim Croce Music Award," initiated by Ingrid to provide scholarships for working musicians.

As our project neared completion, A. J. Croce and Michael Bizar went on national television with the edition guitars to sing one of Jim's timeless songs and to support Katie Couric's charitable efforts toward cancer research. Like "Time In A Bottle," the whole project seemed to capture the essence of Jim Croce, whose music has had such a profound impact.

Above: The Jim Croce Signature Editions shared the same style hardshell denim case (left) and an encapsulated mint condition 1973 dime (right) commemorating the year of Jim's tragic plane crash.

STEVE MILLER 00-37KSM/00-37K2SM
Hawaiian flames for The Gangster of Love

THE PHONE RANG EARLY ONE AFTERNOON.

"This is Steve Miller." The voice on the other end seemed familiar.

"THE Steve Miller?" I asked.

"Yes, I suppose," he answered rather drolly.

He wanted to stop in the following day to see the factory. I said I'd be thrilled to show him around and put it in my schedule. I was a big fan of Steve's and was excited about the visit.

He arrived just after lunch the next day with his wife Kim and a few members of the band. After a thorough tour, Steve wanted to sit down and talk guitars. He ended up ordering nearly twenty instruments — an impressive array of stock models and special customs.

Over the next months, the guitars became available one by one. After I was satisfied that each instrument was up to snuff, I would call Steve to let him know what was ready. He was always excited about the guitars. With each conversation our camaraderie grew until he suggested to me that I should consider coming out to his home in Idaho for a visit. I didn't really take this very seriously until he mentioned it a second and then a third time during our subsequent conversations. I warned him that if he invited me again, I just might take him up on it and he did, and I accepted.

Steve and Kim's Idaho property was fantastic — an incredible house, three adjacent guest cottages, a first-rate recording studio, and an art studio, all situated along a rushing river a few miles north of town. I spent about five days there and we had a great time. We played guitars, recorded some impromptu sessions, talked about guitarmaking, did yoga, hiked, drew, enjoyed great meals, and smoked cigars on the porch. In the months and years that followed Steve and I hooked up often at trade shows or during his summer tours with The Steve Miller Band. It's remarkable how powerful and memorable Steve's set list of hit songs can be in concert.

Steve had always been an avid environmentalist and in 1986, he invited me to meet him in Southern California for Earth Day. Paul McCartney was on the same bill with Steve and I couldn't pass it up. In a matter of days, I found myself backstage at the Hollywood Bowl helping Steve's crew with the soundcheck.

The McCartneys had gourmet vegetarian pizzas and fresh salads brought in for a backstage feast. Steve and Paul had recorded the song "My Dark Hour" together back during the Abbey Road sessions and as a result, they had maintained a friendship. I was hanging out in Steve's tour bus for a few hours before the show, but when I heard the music start up, I felt like going out front. I immersed myself in the show for about a half hour, then went back to see what Steve was up to. When I stepped up into his bus, he had a pained look on his face.

"Where were you? McCartney was here in the bus for the last half hour. He just left. You missed him!"

My one chance to meet Paul McCartney and I blew it. But the concert was memorable, the time with Steve was special, and I got to see Paul McCartney's set from the front row. Several months later,

Steve's band was touring the summer sheds. They had a day off after their Philadelphia gig. Steve and Kim drove up to Nazareth and came to our home for one of my wife Susan's great lunches. There, Steve alluded to the possibility of Susan and I moving out to Idaho to work for him. We were both excited and we made our plane reservations to fly out to look at real estate.

A few weeks before our trip, Susan discovered that she was pregnant with our first child and our nesting instincts won out over any notion of moving to Idaho, but our friendship with Steve and Kim remained strong. We had several other opportunities to spend time together including several days of sailing in the San Juan Islands with fellow musical-instrument enthusiast Ned Steinberger and his wife Denise. There on the rocky sea, Ned revealed his ingenious adjustable neck for acoustic guitars. Ned, Steve, and I spent hours discussing Ned's invention, and the seeds of a Martin/Steinberger adjustable neck collaboration were born.

We also took the opportunity to brainstorm the preliminary specifications for a Steve Miller Signature Edition guitar. After returning to Nazareth, we started producing artwork, churning out jokers and jesters, jet airliners and space cowboys, flying horses and flying eagles. In the end though, Steve decided to mothball all the inlay ideas in favor of an extremely pure design that could stand on its own merits as an instrument. Constructed of highly flamed Hawaiian koa, only 136 guitars were offered: sixty-eight with spruce tops and sixty-eight with koa tops. the number was chosen because that was the year that Steve burst upon the San Francisco music scene. Aside from the internal label, the only direct reference to Steve on the guitar was a very subtle laser-etched joker mask on the front block of the guitar. We did issue a signature "Gangster Of Love" pick as well that is probably pretty rare in the pick-collecting market at this point.

Of course, the guitars were spectacular — they were all snapped up by the music stores in a feeding frenzy, proving that there is still

We started producing artwork, churning out jokers and jesters, jet airliners and space cowboys, flying horses and flying eagles.

integrity in restraint. Robbie Robertson of The Band picked one up and used it to record his part of the nationally broadcast television commercial for The Gap, featuring the Supertramp hit "Give A Little Bit."

Steve's music remained center stage when the US Post Office leased the rights to "Fly Like An Eagle" for their national Express Mail campaign. After the Last Call tour, he took a temporary breather from performing to enjoy life, but has stayed active in the studio and he and Kim remain my very good friends.

The Martin/Steinberger TransAction™ guitar has also come to fruition, though the prototyping was a real challenge for Martin. The neck system allows the player to adjust the neck angle instantly on an acoustic guitar, regulating string action. Adjustment is made simply by turning an easily accessible wheel which resides just inside the soundhole. Neck intonation can also be shifted by means of an Allen wrench adjustment just inside the soundhole. We had high hopes for the model, especially given that Ned's invention makes neck resetting a thing of the past. Furthermore, action adjustments can be made in the store to suit the taste of each individual customer. Perhaps the idea was just a bit too revolutionary for a fairly traditional company, but it was brilliant just the same. As relatively few edition instruments get out into the marketplace, perhaps further interest will be ignited, as the concept certainly has great merit.

Left: The 00-37KSM (Spruce top).
Right: The 00-37K2SM (Koa top). Both of the Steve Miller Signature Edition models were crafted with back and sides of beautifully flamed (or figured) koawood. This highly prized Hawaiian species falls between rosewood and mahogany in its tonality. To maintain the integrity of the instrument, the fingerboard is devoid of any inlay, including the artist's signature.

JIMMY BUFFETT
HD-18JB
Martin meets Margaritaville

JIMMY BUFFETT HAS BEEN PLAYING MARTIN GUITARS for most of his adult life. In fact, when asked in a magazine personality profile about his favorite possession, he answered that it was his old Martin guitar. Long before I was involved with Artist Relations or Limited Editions, fellow Martin employee John Marshall had made contact with Jimmy Buffett. John had done a good job enlisting the advice and endorsement of a number of other key musicians as well, including Steve Howe and Bonnie Raitt. They, like Jimmy, were enamored with Martin's MC-28 Grand Auditorium cutaway that was designed for recording-studio and stage use.

So our relationship with Mr. Buffett was already established by the time the signature models took off. I re-established contact with a call to Jimmy's offices in South Florida. It wasn't very difficult to get a positive response about collaborating on a signature model. After all, he loved his Martins, but his career was in high gear with his recording, touring, merchandising, authoring a string of national bestsellers, and of course catering to an incredibly loyal cache of Parrotheads. In spite of his frenetic schedule, I received a personal phone call from Jimmy while having Easter dinner at my mother-in-laws. We had a nice talk about guitars. He felt pretty strongly that his signature-model guitar should be a Dreadnought, with mahogany back and sides and herringbone trim. That's the kind of practical input I appreciate from an artist. I hooked up with Ed Durruthy who handled licensing for Jimmy, and through him we worked on the details. The early focus of the model was centered on Jimmy's hit song "Margaritaville." I sketched tall bar glasses, ice cubes, slices of lime, lost shakers of salt, and of course parrots galore, but that just wasn't the direction Jimmy wanted to go. He loved the Caribbean and asked that we come up with a simple palm-tree motif, swaying gently in the warm tropical breeze. We did. It was tasteful and elegant, cut delicately from an assortment of lustrous pearl and abalone, and nested under the cove of the Martin logo.

The legendary and original Margaritaville Store and Café is located in the historic Kress 5 & 10 building in Key West. The street address is 424 Fleming. This seemed like a pretty appropriate number for a limited edition so we jumped on it. When the prototypes emerged from R&D, they were just too damn beautiful. I shipped one of the first guitars down to Jimmy and he just loved it. His office called back that day to see whether they could order twenty-five of them as gifts for Jimmy's friends. That's the way the whole project went. The edition just evaporated and we found ourselves in the same situation that we encountered with the 000-42EC Clapton model — wishing that Margaritaville could have been a few miles down the highway,

Left: The Jimmy Buffett HD-18JB Signature Edition combined Martin herringbone styling with mahogany back and sides, and a stylish Caribbean palm complete with coconuts.

LET ME KNOW WHAT YOU THINK ABOUT A BULLET-PROOF LITTLE MARTIN THAT CAN SAIL AROUND THE WORLD IN A BUNK AND NOT WARP.

perhaps at 4240 Fleming! Nevertheless, 424 guitars is a lot of instruments and everyone perceived the project to be a big success. I was especially thrilled to see Jimmy sporting his Martin next to Katie Couric and Matt Lauer during one of NBC's morning concerts.

Jimmy had chosen the W. O. Smith Nashville Community Music School in Nashville as the recipient of the charitable royalties from the project. The school provides music instruction to children from low-income families for fifty cents a lesson with an all-volunteer faculty. The significant donations went a very long way in providing much-needed funds for the building and for instruments.

There was a certain amount of pressure to jump quickly into a second project with Jimmy, but we felt that it would be prudent to take a little breath between projects. During the downtime we had many opportunities to interact with Jimmy by servicing a variety of Martins that had suffered wear and tear from being out on the road. Our emails back and forth were increasingly laced with humor and satire. We had indicated to Jimmy our extreme pleasure with the first project and hinted that the market was ripe for another, if and when he felt that it was appropriate. Several years passed before he became excited about the prospect of making an "offshore" guitar — one that could take some of the punishment of the high seas. We joked about a teak guitar, but frankly the wood is so oily that the glue just doesn't stick to it.

Next to teak, genuine mahogany is one of the most stable woods on the planet. We decided to combine Jimmy's love of trad-itional 12-fret Martins with the durability of a body crafted with solid mahogany top, back, sides, and neck. I had learned from the Steve Miller koa-top signature model that if you offer a non-spruce top model, there will always be customers that want spruce. If we were to offer two models, what could we possibly call them that had

a practical, pertinent, humorous, and tropical connotation? One of my best friends had been out on the high seas and told me about the hubbub surrounding "pollywogs" (those who have never crossed the equator) and "shellbacks" (those who have). It seemed an appropriate analogy — the pollywog could be the spruce top and the shellback, darker and more durable to the salty air, could be the mahogany top.

Jimmy indicated that he wanted his good friend Phil Bennett of The Hinckley Company to get involved. Hinckley makes very high-end boats and Jimmy wanted the guitar to be both boat-inspired and boat-worthy. Phil and I conspired in discussions about life buoys and conch shells, lighthouses and schooners, compasses and anchors. There were so many great ideas for headstock and fingerboard inlays, and Jimmy was not one to stop looking for new ideas. But then, in a flurry of inspiration, the image of a ship's porthole bubbled up to the surface and planted itself firmly upon the wall of the headstock. I envisioned the tropical palm from the first edition slowly receding into the distance through the open brass porthole — a perfect segue from one model to the next. We ordered metalic foil transfers for the porthole itself and Pearlworks experimented with a variety of materials for the receding palm. Green azurite leaves on an ebony island with an Agoya-shell sky and a turquoise ocean created the perfect image, with a mother-of-pearl ship's wheel at the 5th fret to top the whole thing off.

With their graceful 000 12-fret bodies bordered with half herringbone "ship-rope" inlay around the perimeter of the top, the Pollywog and Shellback models are a sight for any sailor's eyes. As this text is written, the prototypes, like tiny tadpoles, are starting to take shape. Charitable proceeds from these two models are slated for donation in support of WINGS Performing Arts in Gulfport, Mississippi.

Above Left: Soundhole and signature detail of the 000-JBP Pollywog. Above right: Through the open brass porthole, the lone palm tree from the first Buffett edition can be seen receding into the distance. Middle: Jimmy Buffett with his most prized possession — a Martin 0-28, circa 1875.

PAUL SIMON OM-42PS/PS2
"Thanking the Lord for my fingers!"

ROGER SADOWSKY HAD PUT ME IN TOUCH with Paul Simon's offices in Manhattan. Several phone conversations with his management followed and Paul was responding positively to the idea of a signature model collaboration with Martin. I was excited by this since I had been a Paul Simon fan from the start. I knew his lyrics inside and out and appreciated the detail he put into his songs. When the opportunity presented itself to drive into New York City to meet with Paul, I seized it. I had heard that Paul possessed an artist's temperament. This, combined with the huge effect he had had upon me, left me nervous in anticipation of our impending visit.

"A winter's day, in a bleak and dark December." Lyrics from every song were swirling in my head as I approached the famous Brill Building were he keeps his offices. It was freezing cold and the wind howled. There was a small grocery store on the corner so I went in and bought two large fresh squeezed orange juices. I was remembering orange-juice lyrics. This would be my peace offering.

I announced my arrival to the security guard and after a phone call upstairs, he showed me to the elevator. I was heavily laden with guitars to show. As I entered, Martia, Paul's receptionist, greeted me and let me know that Paul would be running late. I was invited to make myself at home.

The first Paul Simon Edition was the OM-42PS, an elegant Orchestra Model with a unique neck -shape, tapered narrow (1 11/16") at the nut but left wide (2 1/4") at the 12th fret—an extraordinary guitar for either fingerstyle or strumming techniques.

Marc was speechless. We both sat there staring at each other, our jaws gaping in disbelief, when suddenly I saw the large wooden door begin to creak open slowly like in a Vincent Price movie, Paul's head appeared sideways. A wry smile crept over his face.

"Just kidding!" He hustled through the door, hung his coat on the hook and came over to greet me properly.

We settled into the more comfortable room where we talked guitars for an hour. You can't talk about tone, of course; you have to listen. So Paul decided that a visit to the Martin factory was in order. Several weeks later he and his son Harper came to Nazareth. They had a field day playing dozens of different sizes, styles, and shapes. At the end of the day, the specifications were decided upon and the prototypes were initiated.

Months later, during rehearsals for Paul's Broadway show *The Capeman*, I delivered the prototypes. Nearly six months after that, Paul's personal guitars were ready and I arranged to deliver them personally. He was recording a number of Capeman songs at The Hit Factory. When I arrived, he was sealed up on one of the sound stages with a large group of background vocalists. After about a half an hour, he finished recording and came out to greet me.

Paul played the two signature-model guitars for about fifteen minutes, then set them down and motioned with his hand for me to come into the sound studio. There were two huge mixing consoles. One of the recording engineers was rewinding the recently recorded track from the soothing fifties doo-wop song "Bernadette." Paul asked him to cue up to the beginning of the song with his lead vocal turned off.

As the playback began, Paul picked up his handwritten lyrics, and standing right next to me, he sang the entire song. That was a very special moment.

His office was divided into two rooms of equal size. The one with Martia's desk doubled as a museum for Paul's gold records and Grammy awards. I put my guitar cases down and hung up my coat.

The other was more like a living room, warmer and cozier, with several upholstered chairs and sofas, a grand piano, and an assortment of instruments arranged around the perimeter of a Persian rug.

After allowing the guitar case to acclimate slowly, I unpacked my personal 000-42 that I had brought along to show Paul. It was a very special 12-fret guitar with Brazilian rosewood and Adirondack spruce. I sat on the leather couch next to the front door and began to play. Time passed and Paul's assistant Marc Silag came in to greet me. Leaving the guitar perched on the couch, I joined Marc at the glass meeting table in the center of the room. We talked and waited for Paul to arrive.

Minutes later, the doorknob jingled and the door creaked open very slowly. Paul was dressed in a heavy winter coat that reminded me of the coat he wore in the cover photo of his second solo album. He poked his head in long enough to pull the hood down and away from his head. He saw my guitar on the couch and with one foot in the hallway and the other propping the door open, he reached down for my guitar, picked it up, strummed a chord, and set it back down as quickly as he had picked it up. He wrinkled a frown on his forehead, looked up, and blurted:

"I don't think so!"

He put his hood back up, pulled the door shut with a loud abrupt slam, and he was gone. I looked over at Marc in horror.

"Is that it?"

Background: Paul Simon with the prototype OM-42PS.
Below: Body detail of the PS2 second edition, a short-scale 000 with a sleek neck, an OM teardrop pickguard, and a redesigned signature.

STING SWC/SWB
SmartWood for smart music

DANNY QUADRUCCI IS STING'S EQUIPMENT MANAGER and guitar technician. Danny's best friend and neighbor is John Kurgan. John is a professional musician, amateur luthier, and recording whiz and I met him during one of his many visits to Martin. We became good friends.

Through John and Danny, I proposed a special Martin signature-model collaboration to Sting. Sting was receptive enough to discuss it further, so John made an appointment with Sting's office. On a sunny Thursday morning in March of 1997, I met John near Central Park West and he helped me with my gear. I'd brought a Martin Humphrey nylon string guitar, a prototype Martin acoustic bass, my personal pinstripe electric bass, and an assortment of strings, accessories, and drawings to break the ice.

We entered through a modest door on the first floor. The apartment was paneled tastefully in dark cherry. To our right was a comfortable waiting room with leather couches and chairs. To the left was a simple office setup. Sting's assistant Teresa informed us that he was meditating and would be with us shortly. I set my things down and sank into the leather couch. There were priceless paintings everywhere. Teresa came in and directed us upstairs.

I gathered my paraphernalia and awkwardly started up the elegant staircase to the second floor. At the top, I clumsily readjusted my load, turned to the right and gasped.

"I'll be damned if that's not an original set of Frank Lloyd Wright barrel-back dining chairs."

Being a big fan of Wright's, this was even more impressive than the paintings.

From the next room I heard a voice say: "That's quite astute!"

It was Sting, sitting on a small Persian carpet in the full lotus position. I entered the large living room with my wares and set everything down neatly.

"What's in the box?" he asked, stretching.

"Oh, just some swag." I smiled.

"You don't have any Martin sweatpants in there, do you?"

"Afraid not." I laughed. John helped me get the various instruments out of the cases and Sting inspected and played them all with care. I knew he was an excellent bass player, but I was particularly surprised at his skill on the nylon string guitar. He possessed an obvious charisma and magnetism.

After looking at the instruments, we sat down and discussed the details of a model. It wasn't long before the subject of rainforests came up. I had been one of the founding board members of the Woodworker's Alliance for Rainforest Protection (WARP) so I was well versed on the subject. Sting asked about the status of mahogany and rosewood. I told him that I thought we should avoid using rosewood, but that we had some lovely quilted mahogany. My feeling was that the boycott of mahogany provided greater incentive for burning of the rainforest canopy to create cattle-grazing lands, whereas use of these woods returned money to the local community and showed them the economic value of sustaining their timber resources.

We sat down and discussed the details. It wasn't long before the subject of rainforests came up.

Sting pondered the merits of my argument, and concurring with my basic logic he said: "Well then, let's do it." And we did it. He took great pride in signing his name for me a dozen times on a blank page for the digital signature artwork. We agreed that the charitable royalties from the project should go Sting's personal cause, the Rainforest Alliance. I returned to Nazareth and began solidifying the designs. I spent an inordinate amount of time working on an Amazon tree-frog rosette motif, which I eventually abandoned out of sheer technical frustration and anyway, Sting loved the rosette on his antique Renaissance guitar. Master luthier Michael Gurian carefully replicated this rosette in various shades of wood veneer. Finally, specifications were agreed upon, woods were selected and matched, and two prototypes were initiated.

The prototypes were stunning. John Kurgan and I made arrangements to meet again with Sting in Manhattan. I was very excited when Sting first opened the case and set his eyes upon prototype number one.

"You've done me well!" he said. A few weeks later, I was off to the NAMM Show where the model was introduced to the music dealers and a flurry of media attention began to encircle the project.

Immediately after the show, I received a panic call from Sting's publicist asking about the guitar. I explained the project to her and the logic of using the quilted mahogany but I could hear concern in her

Left: Sting at his New York flat (above left) with the prototype CMHS Signature Model (below left) that never happened. This Page: The SWC Nylon Sting Signature Edition, fully redesigned with responsibly harvested tonewoods certified by SmartWood. The model was based upon the "Millennium" guitar designs of luthier Thomas Humphrey.

voice. There had been some negative chat on the web about Sting's guitar being made of rainforest-unfriendly woods and instead of trying to defend the position, we decided to reconsider the project. Miles Copeland, Sting's manager at that time, called shortly thereafter to discuss cancellation of all of the orders and arrange for the withdrawal of the model from the marketplace. Fortunately, we had only made the two prototypes. Sting called me personally to apologize and to say that he had underestimated the groundswell of public opinion about the use of mahogany. He offered to work with us to try to salvage the project in a newer, more acceptable direction.

So we swallowed our pride and returned to the drawing board. This time, I focused on SmartWood Certified timbers forested in compliance with standards set by the Forest Stewardship Council (FSC). The Sitka spruce soundboards, although uncertified, were reclaimed from logs that were destined to become pulp for baby diapers. We prototyped a nylon string guitar and an acoustic bass. Once again, John made arrangements to deliver the instruments to Sting in Manhattan for his approval.

Sting had just released his *Brand New Day* CD and was rehearsing with his band prior to a lengthy world tour. John and I met up at SIR Studios. There were several rehearsal rooms at SIR, each slightly larger than a basketball court. A full stage was set up along one wall of the studio. Sting was seated on a stool in the center. For forty minutes we sat sipping Earl Grey tea listening to our personal run-through of the tour set list, and then the band took a break for lunch.

"What do we have here?" Sting eagerly opened the oversized acoustic bass case and started thumping out bass rifts.

"Cool!" he grinned. He took it over to the stage and plugged it in. Dominic Miller, the extraordinary guitarist in Sting's band, was fingerpicking on the nylon string and they fell naturally into Sting's country hit "Laughing Through My Tears." It was a special treat to hear Sting play that bass. He used it for the rest of the after-noon, then walked over to say goodbye.

"I'm keeping this one, right?"
"Of course! It's just for you."

STEVE HOWE 00-18SH
Big sound in a small package

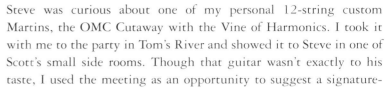

THE 00-18 IS A CURIOUS INSTRUMENT. Between 1898 and 1994, Martin produced more than 22,000 of these small-bodied wonders. That's a lot of guitars. Where could they possibly have gone? It's probable that the people that have them cherish them.

The reason that these 14-fret mahogany guitars were so popular is that they delivered a surprisingly loud, clear and projective tone for a reasonable price. The 00-18s are also comfortable to hold and play, regardless of the stature of the player.

That's what a young Steve Howe must have been thinking when he traded his hard-earned cash for his very first Martin, a 1953 00-18. Like millions of other kids, Elvis Presley's leather-covered D-18 had caught his eye, as did the Martins of his other idols of the time, undoutedly Paul Simon's D-18 and Lonnie Donegan's 000-28 among them.

Steve Howe quickly rose to fame as the groundbreaking lead guitarist for the classic rock groups Yes and later as a driving force with the band Asia. Steve's 00-18 remained his favorite acoustic guitar. He used it to write and record most of the legendary Yes acoustic tracks. Over the years he became an avid collector of acoustic guitars eventually publishing his own book, *The Steve Howe Guitar Collection*. Among the many Martin instruments included were several 00-18s, an SOM-45, a number of Martin ukes, a Style-C mandolin, and a rare 0-28 dating back to 1875.

Steve was no stranger to Pennsylvania. In advance of his many international tours, he would invariably gravitate with his fellow band members to Claire Bros. Ltd., a professional soundstage and rehearsal company located in the small town of Lititz, PA. Nearby in Philadelphia lived Steve's close friend Annie Haslam, most famous for her breathtaking vocal work with the seventies band Renaissance. And up the road in Nazareth, of course, was the Martin Guitar Company.

Martin certainly took notice of Steve's love of their acoustic instruments, photographing him for a national Martin ad proudly holding his MC-28 Cutaway in the early eighties.

After the signature-model projects were well under way in the mid-nineties, I had the pleasure of speaking with Steve on many occasions. We had both been invited to Scott Chinery's gala party celebrating the unveiling of the now-famous Blue Guitars that Scott had commissioned from the upper strata of archtop guitar makers.

Steve was curious about one of my personal 12-string custom Martins, the OMC Cutaway with the Vine of Harmonics. I took it with me to the party in Tom's River and showed it to Steve in one of Scott's small side rooms. Though that guitar wasn't exactly to his taste, I used the meeting as an opportunity to suggest a signature-model collaboration and invited him to visit the factory. Steve's schedule was very tight due to an impending reunion tour with Yes, but he managed to drive up from Lititz on a Saturday morning in January for a visit at my home, as the factory was closed on weekends. At my request, he brought his 1953 00-18 for my inspection. I found the instrument to be wonderful: dry, crisp, powerful, and alive. It was clear that this was the guitar to focus on for the Steve Howe Signature Edition.

He stayed for the afternoon and I showed him instruments from my collection. He played a few of his own arrangements of Dylan songs and we discussed the fact that Dylan had an old 00-18 — he'd been photographed with one for the cover of *Acoustic Guitar* magazine (see page 54.) This was particularly pertinent given that Steve had started working on a Dylan tribute album. We decided on the spot to take a bit of artistic license by adding several sensible upgrades to the specifications of Steve's original 1953 00-18: ebony for the fingerboard and bridge, Engelmann spruce tinted with vintage toner for the soundboard, tortoise-colored bindings, scalloped X-braces, a square tapered headstock, bone nut and saddle, vintage nickel-plated replicas of the original Kluson "oil-hole" tuners, and Steve's signature in pearl above the final fret.

For his charitable royalty, Steve earmarked the Save the Children Federation, a 501(c)3 committed to making lasting, positive change in the lives of disadvantaged children worldwide.

Prototypes were completed and introduced at the Anaheim Winter NAMM Show in January of 1999. Dealers responded favorably by placing orders for more than half of the edition during the show. By the time the edition instruments started to hit the market in June, all 250 guitars were spoken for. While promoting the unveiling of his CD at 8th Street Music in Philadelphia, I arranged to deliver instrument number one of the edition to him there. Steve was thrilled. The project was a complete success, but more than that, the viability of the 00-14 fret design had been fully restored.

The Steve Howe 00-18SH Signature Edition, an upgraded replica of the small-bodied acoustic Martin that Steve has cherished throughout his prolific career.

Right: Dire Straits frontman and guitar virtuoso Mark Knopfler gets down to acoustic songsmithing with his HD-28V, the guitar that provided the basis for his herringbone HD-40MK Signature Edition (left).

MARK KNOPFLER
HD-40MK

Discovering Masiakasaurus knopfleri

PRIOR TO INTRODUCING THE 000-42EC Eric Clapton Signature Edition, I asked Eric's former manager Roger Forrester whether he could recommend an American publicist who would be able to help us effectively spread the word about Eric's signature model. Roger suggested Ronnie Lippin in Los Angeles who has handled Eric's publicity for many years. She agreed to take on the task and did a great job. One day she called and nonchalantly asked: "You want to do a Mark Knopfler edition?"

"Yes!" I replied loudly without any hesitation. Perhaps more than any other musician, I have grown to appreciate Mark's delicate and masterful touch with the guitar. I have purchased every album he's worked on: Dire Straits, Notting Hillbillies, soundtracks, and solo efforts — of course I was interested.

Ronnie had just started to represent Mark and within a few days she had approached him concerning a signature-edition collaboration. The timing was impeccable. Ronnie kept her personal #5 000-28EC Clapton model at work and when Mark picked it up one day he was very impressed. He was also flattered that we were interested in working with him. An evolving conversation about guitar sizes, tonewoods, neck widths, scale lengths, and bracing patterns ensued. I learned quickly that Mark takes his guitars very seriously. Upon request, I shipped a number of assorted models to him via Glen Saggers, his guitar technician in London. Mark pored through our catalogs, books, and literature and gradually homed in on the Vintage Series HD-28V as a starting point for a signature model. In addition, he had spotted an antique rosette design from 1840 that he really loved. I started laying out the tentative specs and creating the digital artwork for Mark's signature while Larry Sifel at Pearlworks tried to figure out how to execute the challenging rosette ring.

Extraordinarily, while we were working on the specifications for Mark's guitar, a team of paleontologists from the University of Utah were experiencing great success finding dinosaur fossils in north-western Madagascar every time they played their Dire Straits CDs. In their own words: "It became our running joke. If we didn't play it, we wouldn't find the fossils, and if we did play it, we would." They decided to honor Mark by naming the previously undiscovered dinosaur species *Masiakasaurus knopfleri*. In the newspapers, Mark responded that he was "delighted and honored" to have a fast-moving, versatile, and vicious creature named after him. I thought this was a great story and proceeded to design various dinosaur inlays for the fingerboard. When this idea was proposed to Mark, however, he didn't seem to respond; reluctantly, I placed the little dinosaur on the back burner.

"MARTIN SENT ME THIS BEAUTIFUL GUITAR WITH ALL THE STUFF I WANTED. IT PLAYED LIKE A DREAM, AND I COULDN'T PUT IT DOWN. I WAS REALLY LOVING THAT GUITAR, SITTING AND PLAYING, WRITING SONGS ON IT AND AFTER A WHILE, I THOUGHT 'WELL, I GUESS I'D BETTER GO MAKE AN ALBUM OF THIS.'"

On route to the annual international MusikMesse in Frankfurt, I arranged to stop in London to meet with Mark personally. Appropriately, he was recording a tribute to Hank Williams, Sr. with his fellow band members and Emmylou Harris at Nomis Studios in Shepherd's Bush. I arrived quietly right in the middle of the session. When they took a break, Mark greeted me briefly and sat me down with a cup of tea right smack in the middle of the studio. After several takes everyone retired to the recording console to review the playbacks. After much rewinding, Mark decided that a few extra tracks of vocal layering were needed, so he and Emmylou headed back into the studio. It was clear that this would take some time. I went downstairs to the cafeteria for some lunch. Halfway through my salad, Mark came to my table and to my surprise pulled up a chair.

With sales of more than 105 million records and discs, Mark is a very significant talent to reckon with. I wanted to get it right. I had a lot of questions that needed resolving in order to finalize the specifications. While eating our lunches we discussed headplate materials, difficulties surrounding the cutting of the rosette squares, then we tackled some last-minute inlay ideas. With great hesitancy, I produced my illustration of the tiny dinosaur and made my final plea for its inclusion.

"I know you don't want this on the fingerboard," I pleaded, "but how about we bury this little critter inside the body, laser etched on the front block above the serial number?"

I waited. A gleam appeared in his eye. "Then everyone can discover the little Knopfleri for themselves, just like those blokes in Madagascar!"

"Exactly!"

Two months later, three prototypes were well underway, the first of which would be Mark's personal Brazilian rosewood guitar. Mark was kicking off the tour in support of his *Sailing To Philadelphia* album release. I had extended an invitation for a factory visit and on a sunny Friday in April of 2001 a chartered helicopter descended upon the Nazareth Speedway.

Mark, with bass player Glenn Worf and guitarist Richard Bennett, hopped into the Martin van for a tour around Nazareth before being whisked over to the factory. The HD-40MK prototypes were assembled to body and neck stage and Mark wished to make some final adjustments to the specifications.

Knowing that these fellows appreciated good cuisine, my wife Susan catered a gourmet lunch that included Calandra's wonderful mozzarella (the locals often say "Cheeses of Nazareth" with a grin), but with the evening's show at Philadelphia's Tower Theater in Philly calling, it was back to the helicopter for what Glenn described as "a walk in the air." I missed the Philadelphia show but was fortunate to catch the Sunday night performance in New York at the Beacon Theater. Quite by accident, we sat next to actress and diva Bette Midler. Bette left the show wanting to know where she could take guitar lessons to learn how to play like that. Mark was simply too good. We couldn't help her.

As the guitars came through one by one, it became clear that Mark's strong convictions regarding how his Martin model should look and sound were naturally inspired: 251 guitars were made and are already cherished by their owners. Several of the instruments found their way into the inspired hands of Mark Knopfler and his band who now have released a largely acoustic album entitled The Ragpicker's Dream. That's where the relevance and satisfaction really are — in placing wonderful tools in the hands of inspiring musicians.

LONNIE DONEGAN 000-28LD
A *salute to the King of Skiffle.*

CHRIS MARTIN TRAVELS A GREAT DEAL and often discovers aspects of international culture that are relevant to Martin guitars. One day he called me in and handed me a chapter of text copied from a book about "skiffle," instructing me to brush up on my British music history. I knew that the early Beatles had formed a group called The Quarrymen and that they were said to be a "skiffle" band, but I must confess that I didn't fully comprehend then what skiffle music was all about.

I read the chapter and learned how American roots music had originated along the banks of the Mississippi and in and around New Orleans. Prior to World War II, American recorded music was confined to big bands staffed with well-seasoned professionals. A grass roots music movement evolved that allowed for homespun instruments like banjos, washtub basses, spoons, and other objects to make more downhome music. "Skiffle" parties were generally held in low-income neighborhoods around the kitchen table. With the war, this unique musical genre found its way to Europe and England through American troops, where it flourished in the hands of a young musician named Anthony James Donegan.

spite of several heart attacks and bypass operations, was full of energy and spirit. After a supercharged performance he received a standing ovation from the crowd that was definitely of Lonnie's "generation."

Lonnie's 1967 000-28 received a thorough and proper inspection and we brainstormed an assortment of elaborate design motifs for his signature edition. Lonnie struck me as a quirky individual, very talented, eccentric, quick-witted, and full of character.

Back in Nazareth, the ideas came to fruition. The fingerboard provided a perfect canvas for some truly unique inlays — a crown signifying Donegan's MBE and "King of Skiffle" status on the 3rd fret, "SKIFFLE" spelled out in stylized pearl from the 5th to the 17th frets, and Lonnie Donegan's name spelled out between the 18th and

"I identified 'Martin' from all the early photographs I saw of blues singers.

I bought my first Martin from a window stall in Walthamstow for six pounds.
I have been using a Martin guitar ever since!"

While backing up blues and jazz legend Lonnie Johnson, an announcer's mistaken introduction got him the nickname "Lonnie" Donegan, and it stuck. Lonnie's driving, accessible amalgam of folk, blues, jazz, and country created in the early fifties resulted in thirty-four Top 30 hits in Britain from 1958 to 1962. More importantly, his earthy, guitar-based brand of popular music inspired a vast array of British musicians including all four of The Beatles, Elton John, Van Morrison, Ron Wood, Cliff Richard, Albert Lee, Rory Gallagher, Albert Lee, and many more. In the simplest sense, he convinced an entire generation that they were entitled to invent their own music.

With the help of Philip York, the Martin distributor in the UK, we were able to contact Lonnie at his home in Malaga, Spain, to discuss the potential for a signature model. Lonnie was incredibly thrilled and suggested that we meet up in England as he was headed out on tour. The Frankfurt MusikMesse was on my schedule and I had already made plans to stop in to visit with Dire Straits guitarist Mark Knopfler in London on my way to the show. With relative ease, I added another day to my trip and arranged to see Lonnie in concert in the small town of Beverly up along the eastern coast. Philip and I took the train out of London and arrived at the quaint little town in time to meet Lonnie for the soundcheck. The old Beverly Theater was packed to the gills. Lonnie, having just turned seventy and in

20th frets. According to his very specific wishes, each instrument was to receive Martin's 1935 dark sunburst finish and be fully equipped with stage-ready electronics.

The headstock combined the Martin gold-foil logo with a rather endearing mother-of-pearl water-rat inlay — the insignia of the Grand Order Of Water Rats, the musician's aid society whose members include Mark Knopfler, Brian May, Eric Clapton, and most every other important musician in the UK. The nonprofit Water Rats would receive the charitable proceeds from the sale of each Lonnie Donegan signature guitar.

Ironically, the success of many young musicians who began in skiffle, including The Beatles and Van Morrison, caused its decline in the sixties. Donegan himself moved from the microphone to the producer's chair, made a brief comeback in the late seventies, then was laid low with heart trouble. Though he rebounded countless times, he finally collapsed on tour in November of 2002 at the age of seventy-one. By coincidence, his last performance was in Nottingham, which was the first city he played as he hit the big time in 1957.

Lonnie Donegan changed the face of British popular music and inspired nearly every major musician alive today. The guitars that bear his name now take on a special meaning.

Above: The Lonnie Donegan Skiffle Group (Lonnie center stage) circa 1957, with his original Brazilian rosewood 000-28.
Left: Detail of the Lonnie Donegan 000-28LD Signature Edition guitar.

MARTIN CARTHY 000-18MC

Martin salutes Martin — a British folk hero gets his due

IN MY HUMBLE OPINION, Martin Simpson is one of the finest guitarists alive in our time. It was my pleasure to meet this fine fellow many years ago when I was operating my notorious Nazareth home, gallery, concert hall, and multimedia art studio, The Church Of Art. Martin performed several concerts there and participated in virtually all the guitarmaking symposia that I had organized as director of the Association of Stringed Instrument Artisans (ASIA). We became very good friends. His musical pursuits took him from England to Upstate New York, then to Santa Cruz and New Orleans. Soon after his return to the UK, he called from me from England to suggest that we consider paying tribute to his good friend Martin Carthy with a signature-edition guitar. I was certainly aware of Martin Carthy's contribution and influence and with Martin Simpson's help, I made quick contact with him at his home in Yorkshire along the east coast of England.

In the months that followed, I immersed myself in Martin's box set *The Carthy Chronicles*. This provided complete insight into his incredible musical legacy. Arguably the most influential folk musician in Britain, his forty years of musicmaking have spanned traditional and contemporary genres, solo, duo, and group efforts, live performances, and a seemingly endless list of recordings. His numerous musical intersections include Dave Swarbrick, Steeleye Span, the Albion Country Band, Brass Monkey (along with John Kirkpatrick), and Waterson/Carthy with his wife Norma and daughter Eliza, herself rapidly becoming recognized as one of England's great musical talents. Paul Simon and Bob Dylan paid close attention to Carthy's music and both of them acknowledge his influence and have integrated his songs into their own work. More recently, Martin Carthy was named Member of the British Empire (MBE) for his services to British folk music.

A 1959 000-18 Martin guitar has been at the core of Martin Carthy's music for most of his career. Well worn from years of heavy play, the small-bodied instrument has taken on that typically dry and crisp sound so characteristic of older mahogany Martins. The most unique aspect of the guitar is the zero-fret modification that was made to the nut end of the fingerboard. This and the addition of three brass bridge pins on the three treble strings produce a piano-like clarity to the notes, especially in the context of Carthy's variety of unusual tunings.

It was a challenge to convince everyone at Martin (myself included) that the zero fret was worth replicating. Thanks to the efforts of Martin's long time friend, Fred Oster of Vintage Instruments, I was able to meet up with Martin Carthy at a show in Philadelphia. After direct exposure to Martin's unique tuning and style of play, plus a thorough inspection of the 000-18, it became obvious that the inclusion of the zero fret would be a critical aspect of our project. Vince Hockey, a

> "You've done me proud, you really have. I played the guitar on a live radio gig last night. The bloody thing was running away with me. It sounded glorious. She truly is a beautiful piece of work."

luthier friend of Carthy's, was extremely helpful in providing close-up photographs and detailed measurements of this unusual feature.

Delighted with the initial prototype, Martin Carthy christened the new guitar on the appropriately named and conveniently scheduled Four Martins tour that combined the talents of four guitar virtuosos: Martin Carthy, Martin Simpson, Martin Taylor, and Juan Martin. In January of 2003, the 000-18MC was formally unveiled, with charitable royalties from the sale of each Martin Carthy Signature Edition guitar designated in support of Amnesty International.

To review the key points of this story, Martin suggested to Martin that a Martin be created to honor Martin. Got that?

This Page: The unique zero-fret modification shown here in greater detail.
Opposite Page: The 000-18MC pays tribute to Martin Carthy's 1959 000-18 right down to the brass bridge pins on the treble strings and the zero fret near the nut.

ERIC CLAPTON

MANY MARTINS

WHILE ERIC WAS OUT ON TOUR supporting his *From The Cradle* album release, he performed the driving rhythm of the song "Motherless Child" with his Custom Martin J12-40 12-string. Around the same time, he appeared in a magazine ad with a Martin Dreadnought in the background. The story filtered back to us that while he had never been particularly fond of Martin Dreadnoughts, a friend had shown him an old vintage D-28 that was so tonally stunning it changed his views about our flagship guitars and he bought it on the spot. He had also picked up an old small-bodied Size-1 Martin in need of refurbishment. The Martin Repair Department went over it with a fine-toothed comb for which both Lee Dickson (Eric's guitar technician) and Eric were most appreciative.

Lee called one day to order a Size-5 Mini Martin so that Eric would have something to play on a fishing vacation in Vancouver. Christie's well-publicized auction of Eric's guitars in support of The Crossroads Centre in Antigua. was particularly interesting with regard to what was not put up for sale, as he kept nearly all his special Martins. The few that he did sell brought extremely high bids, in particular the 000-28 that Eric described as his chief guitar throughout the seventies. It brought in a whopping auction bid of $173,000.

All these occurrences are significant because they contributed to our ongoing relationship and friendship with Eric. Clearly, he was loyal to Martin acoustics and we were thrilled to have such a meaningful and prosperous relationship with him.

The fact that there was tremendous leftover demand for more Eric Clapton signature-model acoustic guitars caused us to consider adding an Eric Clapton stock model to the line, but our policy required that any such offering be significantly different from the previous edition model. Eric responded well to our suggestion of a more affordable model, the result of which yielded some exceptional prototypes of the proposed 000-28EC guitar. This was in effect identical tonally to the 000-42EC model, but without all the pearl and glitz. Simple, classic herringbone rosette and body trim were blended with ivoroid bindings and vintage Style-28 appointments. We sent one of the prototypes to Eric in England and he sent these exact words back through Lee: "Don't get me wrong. I love my 000-42EC Martins. The craftsmanship and detail are superb. But this new 000-28EC model is the best-sounding acoustic guitar I've ever played."

Many thought that the success of these Clapton signature models was the dependence upon the association of Eric's name and reputation and of course there is truth to that, but the fact is that these guitars are indeed as special as the performer that inspired them. There is something magical in the expressiveness of a short-scaled Martin 000. The strings are looser and they can be pushed further than their long-scaled OM counterpart. The tonal balance and visual integrity are the result of specifications that were totally uncompromised and it shows in every one of the guitars. This is not to say that each one is identical; in fact they are surprisingly consistent, but the spruce and rosewood are natural materials with subtle variances. If you line ten of them up in a row and compare them, each will have its own character and voice. Some are slightly punchier. Some are more resonant, but they are all very special.

We took the 000-28EC to the Nashville NAMM Show in July of 1996 and returned home with a slew of orders. Eric had added the 000-28EC to his cache of performance guitars and he continued to be surprised at how a lower-cost instrument could stand up to the top-of-the-line guitars. On the phone one day he relayed that his 000-28s were "utilitarian in the very best sense of the word." For someone so immersed in the blues, "utilitarian" can be a very good thing.

000-42ECB

IN OUR DISCUSSIONS about potential new projects, it seemed obvious that a Brazilian rosewood version of the initial 000-42EC edition would be received enthusiastically in the marketplace. Eric liked the idea of a small edition of perhaps one hundred guitars, though Chris Martin was concerned that there would simply not be enough instruments to satisfy the demand. Of course he was right. We finally settled on an edition of 200 guitars, identical to the 000-42EC in body size and shape, but enhanced with premium-grade Engelmann spruce soundboards and mother-of-pearl bordered abalone snowflake inlays that made for exceptional contrast against the black ebony fingerboard.

We suggested the "alternate torch" inlay pattern for the headplate. This beautiful design was prototyped in 1902 on one of four very ornate 00-45 instruments (see 00-45S "1902" on page 132), but the pattern was nearly abandoned in favor of Martin's simpler torch pattern. It seemed fitting to revive it for this special Eric Clapton edition.

The charitable proceeds from the 000-42ECB project were donated in support of The Crossroads Centre, Eric Clapton's drug rehabilitation facility in Antigua.

Above: Neck detail of Eric Clapton's Custom OM-50. The lavish "Tree Of Life" fingerboard, developed for the long-scale Dreadnought D-50 Limited Edition, could not be easily adapted for a short scale 000, so a Custom OM-50 was designed instead.
Below: Back to back 000-42ECB Eric Clapton Signature Edition guitars, crafted with Brazilian rosewood, much like Eric's original 1939 000-42.

000-28ECB

MY WIFE SUSAN was at the steering wheel and I was sound asleep as we headed up I-81 toward Ontario for our summer vacation. My cell phone was on the dashboard and I nearly jumped through the roof when it rang. It was Eric. I snapped into shape very quickly.

After giving him a progress report on the crocodile case project, which was in full swing thanks to the perseverance of the folks at TKL Case Company, the conversation turned to the next logical steps after the glowing success of the 000-42ECB. We discussed the merits of completing the "suite" of EC editions with a Brazilian rosewood version of the 000-28EC. After a few concerns were answered Eric simply said: "Well I guess we should do it then." He seemed to be enjoying the process of bringing remarkably exquisite guitars to people that really appreciated them.

With an aggressive fixed edition size of 500 instruments, the 000-28ECB drew its inspiration from the incredibly popular Vintage Series stock model, the 000-28EC. As crazy as it might sound, the idea was to create a "working man's" Brazilian rosewood 000 guitar. With a US retail price of $9,999, that's hardly in the budget of the working man, but Martin vintage Brazilian 000s can bring a great deal more, and there are a lot of working musicians looking for guitars that can deliver that level of balance and tone. In order to embellish the model and differentiate it from its Indian rosewood counterpart, we chose herringbone pearl for the rosette, and mother-of-pearl bordered abalone diamond and square inlays for the fingerboard. Like all the Clapton guitars, a subtle integrity lies just beneath the surface, exuding an aura of restrained classiness.

OM-50

AFTER SEEING A COPY of the Martin Custom brochure, Eric decided that he wanted to have a special guitar made. Lee once more acted as the intermediary. Eric liked the looks of the "Tree Of Life" pattern and this was appropriate since Martin was prototyping the very ornate Limited Edition D-50 model. The D-50 fingerboard featured the most elaborate "Tree Of Life" ever conceived. We suggested to Eric that he consider a custom OM-50 Orchestra Model since this would enable the long-scale fingerboard of the D-50 to be used. The headstock and bridge were also chosen, as was the pickguard, though Lee suggested that we modify the pattern slightly to allow for Eric's initials to be concealed among the vines. Eric liked the idea and we initiated the guitar.

When the pickguard came in from Pearlworks it was radiused for the incorrect diameter rosette and it simply didn't work on the lavish triple-ringed soundhole specified for Eric's Custom OM-50. A new pickguard would have to be made. I hated the notion that such a work of art would be wasted, so we decided to create a specially framed soundboard and rosette with the pickguard mounted as a token of our appreciation to Eric. The Martin employees that assisted with this effort really did a wonderful job. The finishing touch was a soundhole cutout of genuine mahogany laser etched to read:

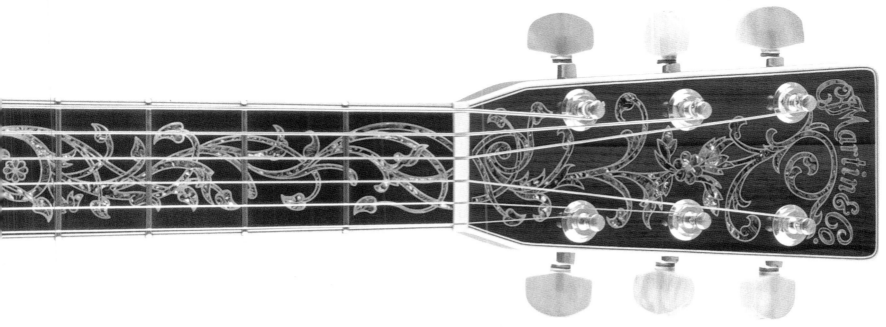

'*This plaque is presented to Eric Clapton by the employees of C. F. Martin & Co. in appreciation of your loyalty to our instruments and in acknowledgement of the great success of the guitars designed in your honor.*'

Coincidently, the OM-50 guitar and the plaque were completed as Eric's 2001 summer tour was in full swing. Our mutual publicist Ronnie Lippin was accompanying the tour and I made arrangements with her to meet up at one of the Madison Square Garden shows in New York City. An hour prior to curtain, Eric called for me. I made my way into his dressing room with the guitar and the plaque. I showed him the guitar and he was taken aback — his only negative comment was that the case didn't live up to the level of detail on the guitar. He asked whether a special case could be made with genuine crocodile skin. I told him we'd look into it. That's another story entirely!

As for the plaque, I think he was quite moved when he saw it. He tucked it away in his personal trunk. Ronnie Lippin explained later that evening that such a gesture from Eric meant that the gift had clearly made an impression.

KATSUYUKI YOSHIDA & HIROSHI FUJIWARA

JAPANESE PEOPLE LOVE MARTIN GUITARS as fervently as they love Eric Clapton. Quality is the bottom line in Japan.

Accordingly, Eric loves Japan as well and has developed several lasting friendships and collaborative efforts there. Two such friends are Katsuyuki Yoshida and Hiroshi Fujiwara. Both are remarkable individuals and avid Martin guitar collectors. During the development of the 000-42ECB model, I was instructed to furnish each of these special friends with one of the edition guitars, compliments of Eric Clapton.

Katsu heads up a company that makes beautifully crafted carrying bags of many different sizes and configurations, including the products of the prestigious Porter brand. Eric loves the Porter bags and has collaborated with Katsu several times. Katsu in turn, has been involved in several guitar projects that reflect the highest

level of appreciation for the guitar maker's craft. Perhaps the best example of this passion is a Martin custom-made "5K" Concert Ukulele with Style-45 vintage appointments, Brazilian rosewood back and sides, and a premium Italian alpine spruce top. This divine instrument rivals C. F. Martin III's flamed mahogany "Daisy" 5K for the position of King of the Ukes!

Hiroshi Fujiwara, a popular cutting-edge musician in the nineties, furthered his fame as DJ. His public image in Japan has evolved into the role of visionary or trendsetter. He seems to have an intuitive golden touch when it comes to elements of design. Hiroshi too has collaborated with Eric on a number of special projects.

In one of his many visits to Japan, Eric Clapton discussed the design of a special Martin guitar with Hiroshi Fujiwara that they now affectionately refer to as the "Black Beauty." Eric called Martin on several occasions to personally discuss some of the ideas that he and Hiroshi had developed. His personal involvement was certainly quite welcome, but unusual given that he often relied on Lee Dickson to handle such details. Aside from an exquisitely polished black gloss finish, the Black Beauty custom specifications called for sterling-silver plated tuning machines specially made for Eric by Schaller in Germany. The tuners arrived and shimmered like pieces of jewelry.

Another very unique element of the Black Beauty was the concentric rosette ring of slotted square inlays in mother-of-pearl. Larry Sifel and Jeff Harding at Pearlworks executed this pattern with their usual passion and attention to detail. The squares formed a full circle requiring that the soundhole end of the fingerboard be hand-radiused to match the rosette arc. Appropriately, the initials of Eric Clapton and Hiroshi Fujiwara were inlaid in pearl at the last fret. Eight of these unique custom guitars were made (six right-handed and two left-handed) and distributed to key friends and associates of "EC and HF." The completed guitars are so stunning that Eric, Hiroshi and Martin are unanimous in wanting to make available a special Black Beauty edition to the general public sometime hopefully in the near future.

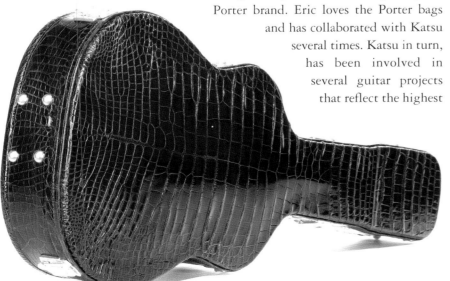

Left: This exquisite case was custom made by TKL Case Company to live up to the special ornamentation of the Clapton Custom OM-50. Right: Katsuyuki Yoshida's custom Style-5 ukulele with alpine spruce and Brazilian rosewood.
Following spread left: Eric Clapton's collaboration with Hiroshi Fujiwara yielded eight very special "Black Beauty" guitars.
Following spread right: A body detail of Eric's Custom OM-50.

KEB' MO' HD-28KM
*Koa meets the blues —
an exercise in understated elegance*

KEVIN MOORE, BEST KNOWN BY HIS STAGE NAME KEB' MO', is a modern-day troubadour of acoustic blues. With his charismatic performing style and fresh, insightful songs, he has expanded the genre in new directions and captured new audiences for a type of music that is both evocative and timeless.

With his career on the rise, Kevin had purchased an austere Martin D-1E in Laguna Beach as a backup guitar. It came to our attention fairly quickly that he was playing a Martin on a regular but non-exclusive basis. We established contact with John Boncimino, Kevin's cordial manager, but it wasn't until several months later, as the summer NAMM Show was wrapping up in Nashville's oppressive heat, that we found ourselves in the same hotel as Kevin — The old Hermitage where both the pro- and anti-suffrage forces of the women's movement had collided. It had also been a favorite celebrity meeting ground for the likes of Dinah Shore, Bette Davis, Greta Garbo, Gene Autry, and Al Capone — quite a group. As we were leaving there was a flurry of activity outside as Keb' Mo's tour bus revved up ready to go. I asked the driver whether Kevin would take a minute to speak with us and moments later we were sitting on the bus together remarking about the Suffragette Historical Marker just outside the window. We exchanged phone numbers and mapped out a basic strategy for our project, agreeing to talk on the phone after we had both returned home. Sure enough, a week later, we were delving into guitars in great depth.

Kevin, tall and lanky, wanted a fairly straightforward and practical guitar with a wider-than-standard neck and a full 14-fret Dreadnought body to compliment his large hands and stature. He didn't want an overly fancy guitar; after all he was known for the blues, but he certainly didn't mind the use of some beautiful woods. He opted for an Engelmann spruce top, prized for its immediate openness of tone. For the back and sides, he was willing and excited to experiment with flamed Hawaiian Koa, reaping the warmth of rosewood and the clarity of mahogany.

Kevin wanted a fairly straightforward guitar with a wider neck and a full 14-fret Dreadnought body to compliment his large hands and stature.

The visual appointments were simple and tasteful — a black ebony headplate complimented the ebony fingerboard with Martin's simple diamond-and-square inlay pattern. The body was trimmed with an abalone rosette and herringbone bordering, and Keb' Mo's stylized signature in pearl at the last fret. When the prototypes were completed we knew we had something special.

Kevin's choice of charities was also refreshing and unique. He stipulated that the charitable proceeds from the sale of his signature guitars be donated in support of the Rocky Mountain Wildlife Center in Boulder, Colorado. With a motto of "A Home for Animals, Not a Zoo for People," the Center has provided assistance for abandoned, abused, and cast-off animals that come from failing or closed wildlife facilities.

A total of 252 guitars were made and quickly sold to an appreciative public, making the Keb' Mo' HD-28KM Signature Model one of the more successful editions offered. Like this special man, the HD-28KM guitar is elegant, professional, handsome, and entirely without presumption.

Above Left: Soundhole detail of the HD28KM. Middle Right: Aside from the dark honey color and beautiful "flamed" grain, Hawaiian koa is prized for its tone that typically falls between mahogany and rosewood. Below Right: Kevin (Keb') at home enjoying his signature-model prototype.

WOMEN & MUSIC
From the parlor to the power chord

BY THE LATE NINETIES, empowerment had found its way to C. F. Martin & Co. in a big way. Chris Martin believed in being open to new management approaches and made every attempt to educate his co-workers about late-breaking hot topics or corporate buzzwords. Many of the employees had offered their individual suggestions about potential limited-edition models, but there wasn't any vehicle for developing those ideas until Chris verbally encouraged the voluntary formation of task teams at one of our company-wide meetings.

Toward that end, one of the first task teams organized was the Women & Music group. The group was comprised, understandably, mostly of women, from a variety of areas: shipping, stringmaking, guitar production and the office. Our enthusiastic clinician Diane Ponzio was a key member of the group and became the natural leader. Many of the women on the task team had not had the opportunity to participate in meetings or projects of this nature and

the process turned out to be beneficial in bolstering their self-assuredness. I sat in, since I was in a good position to advise the group on the elements of guitar specification and design and the procedures for bringing such projects to fruition.

In the early nineteen-hundreds, the majority of guitar players were women. They embraced "parlor-style" music, which they played on small-bodied, gut-string guitars. A close examination of more recent warranty records, a century later, revealed that women were accounting for less than 5 percent of acoustic-guitar purchases. We knew it would take a concerted effort to counteract the trend.

Our challenge would be to take a pro-active role in designing guitars that women would want to play. The Dreadnought is much too unwieldy for most women, yet the smaller-bodied guitars like the 0s and 00s are often perceived, in comparison to the Dreadnought, to be thinner in sound. Eventually the team landed on an idea that

Above: The turn of the century saw parlor guitars in the capable hands of women performers like Vahdah Olcott-Bickford (top), shown here with her quartet.

The five Women & Music models to date have made a profound influence on Martin culture and the music industry in general. The first WAM model was the 00-16DBR (above). The 00-16DBM featured natural mahogany tonewoods throughout (right).

combined the best of both worlds, blending the 00 14-fret Grand Auditorium shape with the full Dreadnought depth. This yielded an instrument that was still comfortable to hold without sacrificing the tonality and projection that serious players demand. The first model was the 00-16DB, with a slotted headstock, mahogany back and sides, and a spruce soundboard. The edition of ninety-seven instruments sold out quickly and received positive media attention.

A rosewood 00-16DBR version soon followed, thereafter a 00C-16DB cutaway, an unusual 00-16DBM mahogany model with a natural finish, and finally a 0016DBFM model in figured maple. Aside from the obvious benefit of selling more guitars, the warranty statistics started to show signs of improvement and Martin's limited-edition collaborations with Joan Baez, Shawn Colvin and the estates of Elizabeth Cotten and Kitty Wells were directly helping to promote female role models.

DIANE PONZIO JDP
"Panache and balance with the engine of a Dreadnought"

IN RECOGNITION OF HER UNTIRING LOYALTY and dedication to the company, longtime Martin clinician and guitar advocate Diane Ponzio was honored in January of 2003 with a special JDP Jumbo Signature Edition.

Born out of her nearly two decades with Martin Guitar, this "clinician's choice" collaboration reflects Diane's experience hosting Martin clinics at hundreds of music stores all over the world, demonstrating guitars at scores of trade shows, and appearing at thousands of her own concerts. There are very few people that possess Diane's passion for Martin guitars or her vast wealth of knowledge about every aspect of the company.

A longtime singer-songwriter, Diane encountered her first Martin during spring break in Berkeley, California. Overhearing what sounded like an orchestra to her, she asked if she could have a try. Playing an E-major chord on the D-28, Diane was instantly "smitten and bitten."

In 1985, a friend suggested that Diane write to Martin to see if they might need a musician to help promote their instruments. With few expectations, she wrote the letter including a tape of her music. Diane was completely shocked when she received a personal response from Chris Martin, who was enthralled with her music and intrigued by the notion of doing Martin clinics with an undiscovered singer-songwriter — one who just happened to be an avowed Martin guitar fan.

Above: New York singer/songwriter/guitarist and longtime Martin clinician Diane Ponzio pursued her dream guitar with her "turbo-charged" JDP Jumbo Signature Edition.

Chris was also keen to promote the newly introduced J-40 model. It seems he chose the right person.

From the onset of her work with Martin, Diane was drawn to the sound, feel, versatility, and look of the J-40. In her own words, the J-40 possesses "the panache of an OM, the balance of a 000, and the engine of a Dreadnought." Accordingly, she has long championed the J-40 as the unheralded gem of the Martin line. Her JDP Signature Edition incorporates personally specified appointments that render it uniquely attractive, collectible, and sonically powerful.

Key features of the JDP model include a three-piece, solid Indian rosewood back offered for the first time on a jumbo body. The spruce top is supported with high-performance quarter-inch forward-shifted, scalloped braces. The resulting sound has exhibited warmth and resonance without sacrificing the balanced and brilliant treble tones. The instrument's visual appeal is accentuated with a unique sunburst top, abalone rosette, and Style-45 inlaid headstock.

The charitable proceeds from the sale each JPD guitar are donated in support of the New York Chapter of The Alzheimer's Foundation, a cause with special significance to Diane due to her late mother's decline from the illness.

Left: Style-40 appointments blended with a black nut and saddle highlight the elegance of a unique sunburst top on Diane Ponzio's JDP Signature Edition.

Right: Face view of Shawn Colvin's M3SC Grand Auditorium Signature Edition.

SHAWN COLVIN
M3SC
The balance of power and elegance

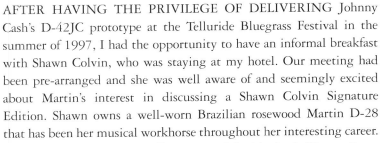

AFTER HAVING THE PRIVILEGE OF DELIVERING Johnny Cash's D-42JC prototype at the Telluride Bluegrass Festival in the summer of 1997, I had the opportunity to have an informal breakfast with Shawn Colvin, who was staying at my hotel. Our meeting had been pre-arranged and she was well aware of and seemingly excited about Martin's interest in discussing a Shawn Colvin Signature Edition. Shawn owns a well-worn Brazilian rosewood Martin D-28 that has been her musical workhorse throughout her interesting career.

Shawn's album *A Few Small Repairs* and the hit single "Sonny Came Home" had just received the 1997 Grammy Award for Best Record Of The Year and Best Song Of The Year respectively. She was flying high with critical acclaim and we talked about her success and her ideas for a signature guitar. She loved her D-28, though she never looked very comfortable with such a large guitar. Primarily a folk musician, Shawn was drawn to the smaller-bodied 000 Auditorium models. She also liked the slightly larger Grand Auditorium "M" models that had become the instruments of choice in the world of singer-songwriters. Both sizes were more ergonomic than the deeper Dreadnought. Her close friend and bandmate John Leventhal had offered to help her with specifications. In fact, Shawn seemed to have a lot of great musician friends that were willing to design a Martin edition for her.

Her life, however, was taking a different turn. Shawn was engaged to be married, was trimming back her touring schedule significantly and, with a new husband and a baby on the way, guitars were not exactly a priority. The project slipped into a state of dormancy. Finally, after several seasons, there were inklings that Shawn was about to re-emerge with a new CD and some performance dates.

Martin clinician Diane Ponzio lives in New York City, not far from Shawn's management offices, and she was more than happy to offer her assistance in resuscitating the project. Her persistence paid off and a simple agreement was signed indicating clearly that Shawn wanted the collaboration to proceed. Nevertheless two small details required resolving: a charitable royalty had not been identified and the specifications for the model remained undetermined.

One afternoon, I received a call from my good friend John Kurgan, who had orchestrated the Sting limited editions. I expressed to him

my frustration that the Shawn Colvin project was stalled. Being very familiar with Shawn's career and music, John felt that he had something to offer and the following day called back with his unique vision of what the ideal Shawn Colvin guitar model could possibly be.

John proposed an M-36 of sorts, constructed with mahogany back and sides, tortoise-colored bindings, a plain ebony fingerboard, and a three-piece back. I jotted all these ideas down and added some of my own. I have always liked the idea of a contrasting the center wedge with the wings of a three-piece back. It seemed obvious to incorporate a rosewood wedge bordered on either side with genuine mahogany. I specified the same motif for the headplate and added an Engelmann soundboard, given that Shawn was born in North Dakota near the stands of spruce that yield these responsive tops.

John Kurgan's ideas had broken the logjam. In a day or two, I faxed the tentative specs to Shawn's office. She was thrilled with the direction and added some interesting touches: ebony tuning-machine buttons and non-invasive Martin/Fishman Gold+Plus electronics. We decided to keep the instrument simple without signature art or fingerboard inlay.

As the prototypes neared completion, the tragedy of September 11 occurred. A few weeks later, I called Shawn's office and suggested that a New York City charity would be very much in order; Shawn agreed and decided that the charitable proceeds from her signature model would be split evenly between the Disaster Relief Fund of the American Red Cross and the Widow & Children's Fund of the Uniform Firefighter's Association.

When the prototypes were completed, we were astounded at how light they were. I have always felt that there is a strong relationship between weight and tone. Certainly, these instruments possessed visual beauty and tonal power, a fitting combination for such a lovely and talented person. When Shawn received her prototype for approval, she was especially stunned and she called personally to say how much she loved the guitar. Apparently she still does because she's been playing it hard on tour and telling audiences the story of how her Martin signature edition came to be.

Top: 3-piece back detail of Shawn Colvin's M3SC showing the rosewood wedge with mahogany wings. Above: Shawn Colvin at home in Texas.

MINI-MARTIN
Reviving the Size-5 parlor guitar

I BECAME INTERESTED IN SMALL GUITARS from the moment I set foot on Martin property. Days after I started working at Martin, I purchased my very first Martin instrument, a T-28 tiple. With the same body shape as the Martin tenor ukulele, the tiple's ten strings are typically tuned in a unique arrangement of two- or three-string courses. The power of this little instrument was astounding to me, but I quickly modified my bridge and nut to create a baby 12-string without the two low E-strings.

Martin historian Mike Longworth shared my fascination with small instruments. In his office, he had a tiny 6-string guitar made with the tiple scale length and body size. Four of these "quartersize" guitars had been made in 1975. In 1981, a dozen more were specially ordered by David Nichols of Custom Pearl Inlay. David was doing virtually all Martin's specialized Custom Shop inlay work, and had a decent Martin dealership going as well. He and I were both enamored by this smaller size and we both made tiny quarter-45s for ourselves in our home shops, complete with quarter-sized snowflake inlays.

In 1980, Martin Quality Control manager John Arndt and I embarked on the design of a 7/8 sized guitar. We simply decided to multiply every dimension by .875 to scale the instrument down to size. I initiated the prototyping process by placing my order for a Custom Shop 7-42 and thus the Baby Dreadnoughts were born. For several years they sold well, the 7-28 and the 7-37K being the most popular. I continued to collect and make smaller-than-standard guitars, thinking of them as "apprentice pieces," much like the miniature violins that were required of apprentice luthiers in centuries past. Nevertheless, I came to the realization that the quartersize guitars were simply too small to play with any degree of comfort. Conversely, the 7/8 size guitars were too large to take advantage of the glassine tonality that little guitars can have. I focused my search on the logical midpoint, the Martin Size 5. Eventually I found a simple but lovely 1963 model 5-16 with mahogany back and sides and a spruce top. It was clearly the best of both worlds: comfortable to play yet still extremely viable with a staccato, almost piano-like tone. I was sold.

Above Left: Another of Martin's historical small instruments, the Baby Ditson, influenced the subsequent design of the larger Dreadnought guitar that would become Martin's flagship. Right: The author's love of turn-of-the-century Size-5 "Terz" or parlor guitars led to commissioning of this Custom 5-41. Opposite Page: The simpler Mini-Martin, shown in proportion to a full-sized Dreadnought model, was fashioned like a Vintage Series herringbone 28, enhanced with the addition of a Style-45 abalone pearl rosette.

Eric Clapton bought one to take on a Canadian fishing trip, Steve Miller took a pair for recording, and Sting gave one as a gift to Bruce Springsteen.

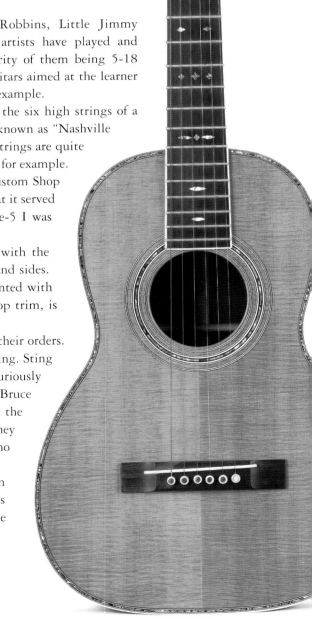

C. F. Martin & Co. first cataloged a Size 5 Martin guitar in 1898. One of Martin's great historic designs, the "parlor guitar," as the popular instrument was known, was played in large part by women of society to entertain their houseguests. By the time Martin slowed production of this fashionable instrument thirty years later, during the Depression, more than 8,500 of these had been sold.

The Martin Size 5 has a scale length of just 21 3/8 inches. With such short scale lengths, the strings can be stretched tighter, producing higher pitched notes as on a mandolin. Tighter strings also yield significantly greater volume.

Size-5 guitars came to be known as the "terz" guitar ("terz" meaning third), because the instrument was invariably tuned a minor third or three half-notes above standard guitar tuning: G, C, F, Bb, d, g. This tuning is identical to placing a capo at the 3rd fret.

Michael Hedges, Will Ackerman, Marty Robbins, Little Jimmy Dickens, Dolly Parton, and many other key artists have played and recorded with Size-5 Martin guitars, the majority of them being 5-18 designation. More recently, several guitar makers have capitalized on the concept of smaller guitars aimed at the learner and travel-guitar markets. The Martin/McNally Backpacker collaboration is of course a prime example.

These little guitars lend themselves extremely well to the use of high strings. By isolating the six high strings of a 12-string set (with sensible experimentation with string gauges), this arrangement, typically known as "Nashville tuning," yields a sweet and clear chimelike tone like that of a harpsichord. In recording, high strings are quite valuable in laying down the treble tracks as proven effectively on Paul Simon's album *Graceland,* for example.

I dusted off the old Size-5 wooden templates and patterns and commissioned the Martin Custom Shop to make a 5-41 with mostly vintage features. That instrument turned out to be so spectacular that it served as the prototype and inspiration for the special edition Mini-Martin. As advocate of the Size-5 I was flattered to join Chris Martin in co-signing the edition label.

The specifications of the Mini-Martin would perhaps be closest to a Vintage Series 5-28 with the addition of a fancier Style-45 abalone rosette. East Indian rosewood was chosen for the back and sides. The solid Sitka spruce soundboard is braced with delicate quarter-inch scalloped braces and tinted with golden "vintage toner." The body, bound in grained ivoroid with fine pattern herringbone top trim, is lacquered and polished to a high gloss.

Introduced in January of 1999, Stephen Stills and Neil Young were among the first to place their orders. Eric Clapton bought one to take on a Canadian fishing trip. Steve Miller took a pair for recording. Sting ordered one and fell in love with it. One day in his studio, a visiting Bruce Springsteen curiously examined Sting's Mini-Martin. It was strung with high strings and tuned a third above pitch. Bruce didn't understand the tuning and started to adjust the tuning gears. Sting, knowing that the sensitive instrument was in perfect tune, jokingly chastised Springsteen for messing it up. They both had a good laugh at this and the next day Sting ordered one as a special gift for Bruce who loved the gift. Months later, Springsteen's office ordered a second one to have "on hand."

Nearly 250 of the Mini-Martins have been sold as of this printing, leading to the introduction of the simply appointed, more affordable 5-15 and 5-16GT models. It is likely that other models will emerge to revitalize the presence of this and other historically significant smaller sizes to the Martin line.

DAVE MATTHEWS DM3MD

The dramatic juxtapositioning of African padauk and Indian rosewood

BY LATE 1997, Larry Dalton of Fishman Transducers had developed an endorsement relationship with several members of The Dave Matthews Band, including Dave himself, and thought there might be an opportunity for Martin — especially given that Dave's friend and acoustic cohort, Tim Reynolds, was a dyed-in-the-wool Martin player. With the gentle influence of Tim and Larry, it didn't take long for Dave to warm up to the idea of doing a Martin signature edition.

Dave's career was taking off like a wildfire, so we didn't want to waste any time in getting the agreement signed and the design process initiated. Dave's right-hand man and road manager Robert "Monk" Montgomery moved things along by ordering a D12-28 12-string and a Vintage Series HD-28V for Dave, both stage-equipped with the onboard Martin/Fishman Gold+Plus Pickup System. Dave loved the guitars, and our timing turned out to be flawless. He had just begun a string of acoustic tour dates with Tim Reynolds that incorporated the use of several Martin guitars, in particular Dave's HD-28V and Tim's special-effects enhanced D-35.

By carefully blending Dave's favorite aspects of these two Dreadnought models, we were able to develop the specifications for the "DM3MD," a clever palindrome referring to the Dave Matthew's 3-Piece-Back Martin Dreadnought. A primary visual aspect of the design was the use of dyed red wood fiber in the inlay lines of the binding and abalone pearl enhanced rosette. In addition, the selection of the naturally crimson-colored African padauk for the center wedge of the three-piece back provided a bold contrast to the purple-brown hues of the East Indian rosewood "wings." The use of padauk seemed especially appropriate given that Dave was born in South Africa. An unusual three-piece headplate with a matching paduak center wedge was created to compliment the unique design of the back.

With a soundboard of Engelmann spruce, the tonality of the DM3MD seemed ideal for the type of aggressive acoustic rhythm-guitar style that Dave Matthews had come to exemplify.

At the time we had no clear comprehension as to just how popular Dave Matthews would become, and the edition size was set at what we thought was an aggressive 234 instruments. By the time the guitars began to arrive in the hands of the Martin dealers, Dave had attained unparalleled popularity, especially on college campuses. The waiting list for each of the 234 edition instruments was ten customers deep!

For all practical purposes, we were proud of our success, but the Peter Principle began to work its magic on the project. Through one of his assistants, Dave had designated The Horton Foundation as the recipient of the charitable royalties from the sale of each edition instrument. In order to proceed with the distribution, I needed the contact information for the charity. After several unsuccessful attempts at getting the details from Dave's management, I took the bull by the horns

and did a quick search on the Internet. I got a quick match on The Horton Foundation and swiftly contacted them to impart the good news. The nonprofit foundation was a suicide-prevention hotline for teenagers and they were naturally very thrilled at the impending windfall — so much so that they asked for the address of Dave's management to thank him in writing for designating their very worthwhile operation. When Dave's office received the letter they were

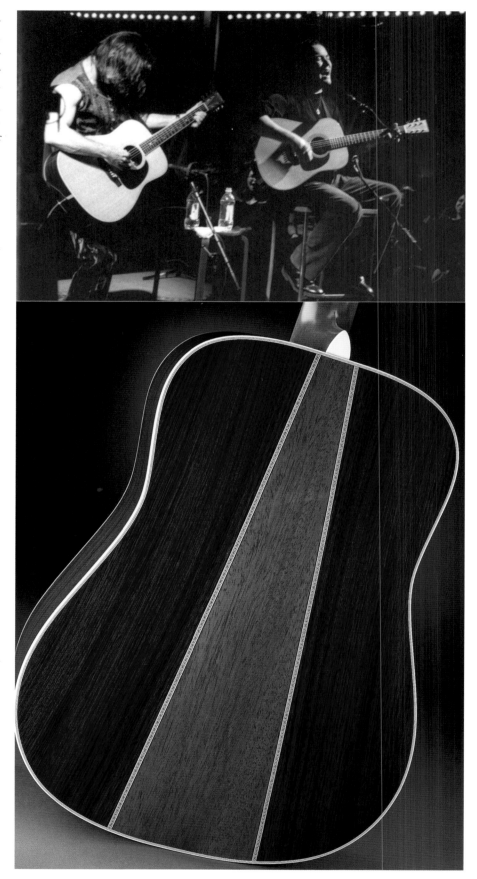

Top: Tim Reynolds (left) and Dave Matthews (right) pair up for a supercharged acoustic tour with their respective Martin Dreadnoughts.
Above: The vivid contrast of African padauk with wings of East Indian rosewood seems fitting for a South African born singer/songwriter.

understandably confused. It turned out that there were in fact two completely unrelated Horton Foundations and I had notified the wrong one — it took a watershed of apologies, a great deal of finesse, and an equivalent amount of capital to rectify my error. A compromise was reached to distribute some funds to both charities. That is the last time I'll entrust any foundation research to the World Wide Web.

As for his signature model, we received a call from a designer who was working on Dave's tour bus. He wanted exact dimensions of the DM3MD so that he could custom-fabricate a special enclosure onboard the vehicle. Hopefully there, as the wheels hit the asphalt, new and original lyrical rhythms will emerge to extend the already impressive legacy of this talented and influential musician.

BECK D-16BH
Thinning the Dreadnought depths

BY THE ARRIVAL OF THE NEW MILLENNIUM, Beck Hansen had been breaking traditions with his edgy, audacious style. Drawing on hip-hop, folk, punk, rock, rap, psychedelia, pop, and blues, Beck was writing, performing and recording an eclectic, postmodern mix of music both uniquely powerful and impossible to categorize. As his visibility increased, it became clear that Beck was a loyal Martin player and that he was having a very dramatic impact on new acoustic music.

As a logical extension of the efforts put forth by the Contemporary Artist Task Team, we put out feelers in Beck's direction and soon established a rapport with John Silva, Beck's manager at the time, and with Shauna O'Brien, John's assistant. Shauna was helpful in conveying to Beck our desire to work with him on a signature-model project and arranged for me to speak with him on the phone. Beck had collected several Martin instruments throughout his career: a late 1990's D-28, a herringbone HD-28V, and an old 000-18, but his favorite guitar by far was his well-worn but tonally powerful D-28, made in 1935.

He explained that with his new album *Mutations* pending release and his very aggressive performance schedule he would not have the luxury to spend a great deal of time conversing about guitar design. This he would entrust to me, but he did have some very clear preferences. He liked his Dreadnoughts for their power and volume but, finding them a bit uncomfortable, asked whether we had ever considered offering a non-cutaway Dreadnought with the thinner 000 depth. There was some precedent for this: I had in my possession a 1960s era Don Thompson/John Huber D-28 prototype, the body of which had been cut to half its standard depth on the bandsaw.

A new back had been fitted, yielding an extremely thin, comfortable body. We discussed the 000 depth option at length and he asked whether the idea had ever been offered: it hadn't, and given Beck's fervent desire to be different, this was the right path to pursue.

He wanted a no-nonsense, stage-ready instrument with onboard electronics that was easy to play, comfortable to hold, resonant in tone, and classy without being gaudy. His hope was that the guitar would cost out at a price range that would be attractive and affordable to the younger players that constituted his fan base. Lastly, he wanted his "Beck" insignia hand-drawn for inlay in the fingerboard, as opposed to simply having his signature replicated.

Beck had furnished all the necessary input and our subsequent work was relatively easy, though there were delays due to Beck's frenetic tour schedule. After a year of slow progress, the prototypes came together and one was sent to Beck for his scrutiny and approval. With so much time having elapsed, the guitar's arrival took him by surprise, but he was thrilled and called to tell us so. That guitar is now part of Beck's corral of Martin instruments. He regularly shows up on stage with it.

Ninety-nine of these special guitars, co-signed by Beck and Chris Martin, were crafted and delivered in their unique faux alligator-skin cases. The charitable proceeds from the sale of each instrument were donated in support of the World Literacy Campaign, addressing the problems of poverty, ignorance, disease, and substance abuse of the world's children through literacy programs.

The edition seems to have become a fitting symbol of Beck's inherent and fresh blend of the radical and the traditional.

Beck's hope was that the guitar would cost out in a price range that would be attractive and affordable to the younger players that constituted his fan base.

Top: Beck with his 1935 D-28. Above: The prototype for the D-16BH Beck Signature Edition combined Dreadnought shape with the thinner 000 depth.

JONNY LANG
JLJCR
The crest of the new wave

MANY OF THE PROJECTS that I was initiating were honoring older, seasoned musicians, mostly white and mostly male. These collaborations appeal to the fans of those artists — the children of the postwar baby boom — but obviously that market will gradually dissipate with time. The new wave of guitar buyers will consist of the children of the Woodstock generation and theirs behind them. It is critical to plant seeds with these future buyers by recognizing young musicians with staying power.

To address that need, a group of younger Martin employees formed the Contemporary Artists Task Team. Their mission was to research, identify, and recommend up-and-coming new artists for potential limited-edition signature-model projects.

With minimal assistance, the team initiated their debut project with nineteen-year-old blues virtuoso Jonny Lang, the youngest guitarist ever to be honored by Martin with a signature edition. Jonny Lang displays such talent that it seems certain he will be around for many decades to come. Listed in Newsweek's Century Club list of the one hundred Americans expected to be influential in the new millennium, Jonny swept the category for Best New Guitarist in *Guitar* magazine's readers poll and made a cameo appearance in the film *Blues Brothers 2000*, performing with Wilson Pickett and Eddie Floyd. He also appeared at the Rock And Roll Hall Of Fame induction ceremony with Jeff Beck. After B.B. King invited Lang to perform with him at the White House, B.B. said "He's got youth and talent. He is starting at the height that I've reached. Think what he might do over time." Lang's second album, *Wander This World*, has already sold over a million copies worldwide.

Designed by Jonny as a recording-studio and performance guitar, the JLJCR is a jumbo 14-fret cutaway with Martin/Fishman® onboard electronics that enable the combination of an undersaddle pickup with an internal condenser microphone. Aside from being stage-ready, the overriding theme of the JLJCR is its aged amber hue, its pearlescent amber hollow hexagon fingerboard markers, and, for the first time ever, a silver Martin logo on the headstock.

All 111 instruments in the edition sold through. The charitable proceeds from the sale of each JLJCR guitar were donated in support of Camp Heartland, dedicated to enhancing the life of children affected by HIV and AIDS.

Background: Jonny Lang wasted no time incorporating his signature model into his live blues performances. Left: The JLJCR combines the jumbo shape with a rounded cutaway and onboard electronics — a serious stage and studio guitar.

SUGAR RAY DSR
Calling on the dogs

THE BAND (NOT THE BOXER) SUGAR RAY came into our radar early in their career. We knew they were Martin players, that they were cutting-edge and talented, and that their videos were getting a good amount of airtime on MTV and VH1. When their management called to purchase some instruments for radio promotions, we selected and expedited the guitars knowing that the exposure would be valuable. The band members liked the no-frills functionality of the more affordable Road and X Series instruments like the DM and the DXM, but they also purchased one of the pristine Eric Clapton 000-28EC signature models.

With our relationship developing and their popularity growing, we began a phone exchange about a Sugar Ray signature edition. Their manager Chip Quigley responded well to the notion and conveyed the proposal to the individual members of the band. Guitarist Rodney Sheppard was the most excited at the prospect. He took charge and became our primary liaison.

During the Anaheim NAMM Show in January of 2002, Martin Artist Relations associate Chris Thomas met up with Rodney and Matt Baratto, the band's gear manager at the time. Martin had just introduced the ALternative X guitars and Chris was intent on getting one of these flashy aluminium-topped acoustic/electrics into Rodney's hands to use at the Pro Bowl halftime show in Hawaii. Rodney was impressed with the guitar and he took it with him, but the model just didn't mesh with the image and direction the band wanted to take. They aspired to simple, no-frills, all natural wood guitars.

In the meantime back at the factory, one of our co-workers, Nate Condomitti, had initiated his order for a special Custom Shop guitar. The model was basically a mahogany-topped Jumbo 12-string (J12-15), but Matt wanted to bullnose the perimeter of the top and the back with the radiused router bit that had been used on the holographic "Concept" guitars. It was a great idea and soon the instrument found its way to the Artist Relations office. We were searching for something bold and new to propose to Rodney Sheppard and this was just the ticket.

In a flurry of creative energy, inspired in part by Rodney's dog and Sugar Ray's mascot Austin, we generated an assortment of canine themed inlay art: a bulldog for the headstock, paw prints for the fingerboard and a bone to mark the octave. All the inlays were executed in green ripple pearl including the stylized "Sugar Ray" logo that appeared at the last fret.

Chris Thomas, a genuine fan of the band, took charge of the project and arranged to take several instruments up the road to Stroudsburg to intersect with Sugar Ray's winter tour. Backstage after the show, the band members checked out Matt's J12-15, the proposed inlay drawings, and a sample of our proposed burgundy-red finishing panel. There was complete consensus among the band members who unanimously opted to sign all the interior labels of the edition. Sugar Ray bass player, Murphy Kargas added his playfully cryptic and personal comments to most of the labels as encouragement for any would-be edition owners.

The guitar was very cool — perhaps a bit too cool for our more conservative customers, but a respectable fifty-seven instruments sold. Sugar Ray in particular loved the guitars; in fact everyone in the band acquired one. So did their manager, their guitar tech, and even their webmaster. Sugar Ray performances incorporate the edition instruments in a big way.

In the midst of our production, we received a call from a number of "Bulldog" fans from the University of Georgia. It seems that the notorious football team shares much of the canine logo art and some of the fans were interested in the guitar. The dog theme, too, was carried to even further limits with the band's cameo Hawaiian luau appearance in the motion picture Scooby Doo. Great timing! Go figure!

Above Right: Sugar Ray guitarist Rodney Sheppard on stage with his DM. Below Right: The all-mahogany Sugar Ray DSR with bulldog, paw prints, and an octave bone.

BABYFACE
000C-16RB
A lefthanded Venetian cutaway, strung "righty"

WHEN THE 000-28EC WAS LAUNCHED, Eric Clapton was very proud of his signature model. It wasn't unusual to get instructions from Eric's office to ship instruments to an assortment of musician friends and collaborators. For two such gifts, he asked that a special note be included in each case pocket to let the recipient know the nature and source of the gift. Given that the gifts were going to two very special performers, Robbie Robertson, former frontman of The Band and singer-songwriter-producer Kenny Edmonds ("Babyface"), I couldn't resist composing a short humorous verse to accompany each guitar. It started like this.

Because of your collaborative interaction
with a certain guitar player named Eric Clapton,
he's sending you this glorious contraption
accompanied with this dubious caption.

We were delighted that "Babyface" had been exposed to Martin guitars during his friendship and collaboration with Eric Clapton. The more we learned about his musicianship and talent, the more impressed we were. As of the year 2000, he had been honored with ten Grammy awards, including Producer Of The Year for three years in a row. With 119 top-ten R&B and pop hits, forty-seven number one R&B hits, and fifty-one top-ten pop hits — including sixteen number ones — his efforts had produced sales of over thirty million singles and eighty million albums. He has written and produced hit songs for many of contemporary music's most popular superstars, including Boyz II Men, Madonna, Whitney Houston, Mariah Carey, Michael Jackson, Lionel Richie, Mary J. Blige, Faith Evans, Toni Braxton, Celine Dion, Aretha Franklin, Vanessa Williams, TLC, and Eric Clapton. It became obvious to us that Babyface was extremely deserving of an edition and that such a collaboration would expose Martin to a completely new musical genre.

Our direct conversations with Babyface yielded specifications for the 000C-16RB Babyface Signature Edition, an economically priced, rounded Venetian cutaway inspired by Eric's 000-28EC, but with a number of alterations and enhancements. Rare, Italian alpine spruce of the same species used for Antonio Stradivarius's violins was selected for the sounding board, and the soundhole rosette was inlaid with highly colorful abalone pearl. The 000C-16RB remains a very contemporary and practical instrument, and like the MC-28, it is ideal for use on stage and in the studio. Introduced in January of 2000, all one hundred of the edition guitars sold to very appreciative and lucky guitarists.

Babyface is a left-handed player who, like many lefties (such as Elizabeth Cotten), learned to play using right-handed instruments turned upside-down. To accommodate his unusual playing style, Babyface's personal-edition instrument is a left-handed cutaway, strung "righty." With respect for lefthanded players, the edition was offered in left- or right-handed versions at the same price, a precedent that is now standard across most of the Martin line.

As a finishing touch, the charitable proceeds from the Babyface guitars were donated in support of The United Negro College Fund, the nation's oldest minority higher education assistance organization.

Above: Eric Clapton and Babyface in a thoughtful moment during their collaborative recording sessions. Inset: 'Bookmatched' Babyface signature models — lefty and righty!

KENNY WAYNE SHEPHERD

JC-16KWS

Blue on black
with pearl bordered lapis tears

KENNY WAYNE SHEPHERD CAME ONTO OUR RADAR through our publicist Ronnie Lippin. At the time of our first contact, he had been in the music spotlight for just five short years, demonstrating his guitar mastery on everything from Delta slide to Texas blues rock, with singles and albums crossing over to become mainstream hits. After the release of his first album, *Ledbetter Heights*, he hit the big time and moved from clubs to stadium gigs, opening for the Eagles and Bob Dylan.

His second album, *Trouble Is...*, remained at the top of the *Billboard* magazine blues chart for two years and yielded three number 1 radio singles. His *Live On* album, released late in 1999, continued the winning streak with the single "Last Goodbye" becoming a major hit in 2000.

Like Jonny Lang, Kenny Wayne is an electric player who found some inspiration in acoustic experimentation. And, like Jonny, he was flattered at Martin's interest in his music. He had picked up a Martin SP000C-16E cutaway model and had found the basic size and shape to be comfortable. In addition, he considered the onboard electronics critical to his particular stage needs.

We quickly started the process of designing a model, based on his 000 but edging up a size to a Jumbo. One of his bigger hits was the song "Blue On Black" and it provided the imagery and the inspiration. I clearly envisioned an instrument with a brilliant translucent blue

lacquered top with black sides, back, neck, and trim, blue paua rosette pearl and fine blue inlay lines. Kenny liked the ideas and added pearl-bordered blue lapis "tears" as the fingerboard position markers.

The prototypes of the JC-16KWS were simply astonishing. When we conveyed our excitement to Kenny, he expressed a desire to attend the unveiling at the 2001 Anaheim NAMM Show. He gave an impromptu performance at the Martin Dealer Dinner on his brand new guitar, christening it with several fresh playing scratches, then joined Merle Haggard in the booth the next day for some more jamming and autographing.

The "blue on black" appointments certainly were appealing. Martin dealers responded with 198 orders that challenged Martin's finishing department for several months. The charitable proceeds from the project were appropriately targeted for The Providence House, a shelter and development program for homeless families with children in Kenny's home town of Shreveport, Louisiana.

This page: Kenny Wayne Shepherd's SP000C-16E (above) provided a good basis for the development of the larger JC-16KWS (upper right).
Following page (left side): "Blue on black" JC-16KWS top detail.

CONCEPT GUITARS CONCEPTS 1 & 2

From pace cars to stage guitars — breaking away

CHRIS MARTIN LOVES CARS. It can't be put any simpler than that. His father loved cars too — fast ones. Even C. F. III had an appreciation for a good set of wheels, driving a fine Mercedes. Cars possess prestige, personality, panache, and polish much as quality guitars do.

While Nazareth is widely known as the home of Martin guitars, Mario and Michael Andretti live here too and Roger Penske's Nazareth Speedway circles the south end of town. The annual Indy Car and NASCAR races provide a convenient vehicle for Chris's love of the automobile and few races run without Chris in attendance.

One sunny afternoon prior to a major CART race, we were checking out the many corporate exhibits that surround the track when Chris happened upon the PPG Pacecars, which were finished with breathtaking holographic lacquer. We were all amazed at how the suspended metallic pigment could change so dramatically when viewed from different angles. Chris was immediately captivated and he inquired about the unusual finish. At Chris's prodding, Tim Teel in Martin's R&D Department followed up with PPG the following week and soon we acquired some of the holographic finish at the incredible cost of $4,300 per gallon. OSHA regulations were stringent on this unusual material, requiring that they be sprayed in isolation of any other finishing processes. Achieving the finish was a major challenge, but we felt the result would be flashy and impressive, especially on stage.

In order to truly take advantage of the visual effect of the finish, it was necessary to create a nonporous surface without sharp edges or need for wood filler. The result was the first stage-ready acoustic/electric Martin "Concept" model with a fully contiguous cutaway body, created with maple back and sides, a spruce top, and gently bull-nosed edges devoid of any bindings. The Concept model drew much attention at trade shows, especially from the media. While the high price-tag limited the number of viable customers, the guitars served to surprise the musical community into the realization that, as a company, we were prepared to unleash some bold ideas heretofore rarely displayed from such a traditional firm.

A second Concept II model followed, equally expensive and challenging. Eventually we cried "uncle" in the face of the manufacturing difficulties associated with the finish, but some great-looking stage guitars made it into the hands of a limited number of lucky performers, and the invisible door between technical curiosity and innovation had been quietly unlocked.

Previous Page (right side): Top detail of the dramatic Concept I Jumbo Cutaway with contiguous edges, stage-ready electronics, and cyan to magenta holographic lacquer.
This Page (left): Full view of the Concept I with hollow hexagons and matching headplate. The 000-Cutaway Concept II (right) followed with magenta to gold lacquer.

MTV UNPLUGGED MTV-1/MTV-2

A groundbreaking TV show inspires a groundbreaking guitar

WHEN MTV LAUNCHED the groundbreaking *MTV Unplugged* in 1989, we at Martin didn't really have any sense of the impact that the show would have upon our company, let alone the entire acoustic-music market. From our standpoint, it seemed ironic to have a show based on an "unplugged" premise — the term itself seems to imply that the normal state of the guitar is to be "plugged in" and that somehow this "unplugged" concept was a new phenomenon. We had always been "unplugged" and proud of it!

The concept for the show was to enlist popular musicians that were typically associated with amplified music and show their talents in an intimate, almost coffee-house setting. It was a tremendous success largely because the acoustic format was able to reveal true talent much more effectively than in the often concealing barrage of loud electric noise, effect, and distortion.

An interior edition label displayed the mutual company logos, the signature of Chris Martin, and the edition number. MTV and C. F. Martin agreed to match equal portions of the charitable proceeds from the edition in support of LifeBeat, a music-industry AIDS awareness and resource organization.

Van Toffler, Executive Vice President of Program Enterprises explained that "*MTV Unplugged* is about the artist and music in a stripped-down setting, We created an *MTV Unplugged* guitar to give fans of the show an opportunity to make their own music with a versatile and meticulously crafted instrument. We chose Martin guitars as our partner because they are the leaders in creating quality guitars, with the best materials using expert craftsmanship."

We sold 697 MTV-1 Limited Edition guitars, significantly more than any other Martin edition with the exception of the 000-28EC

The repair department had built an odd sample guitar to show off their talents on an instrument that displayed many disparate styles. This guitar provided the seed of inspiration for the MTV-1 project.

It became increasingly difficult for the *MTV Unplugged* show to escape our attention. The presence of Martin guitars was evident on a good percentage of the performances. Furthermore, there were bands that had so little experience with acoustic guitars that Alex Coletti, the show's bold producer, was prompted to contact Martin often to request quality loan instruments. Gradually, we established a friendly and symbiotic relationship with Alex. With the airing of Eric Clapton's stellar *Unplugged* performance, the whole world took notice. The ultimate result of the show's success was a rekindling of interest in acoustic music, followed by a definite resurgence of acoustic-guitar sales, and the now-obligatory inclusion of the acoustic set in virtually every rock band's set list.

It's hard to gauge the exact effect of *MTV Unplugged* upon guitar sales but there was little question that we benefited tremendously. It seemed obvious that any collaboration would be fitting and gradually our conversations with Alex turned into trips back and forth from New York City to Nazareth.

During the same time period, the Martin Repair Department had built an odd sample guitar that was an amalgamation of many different tonewoods, binding colors, tuning gears, and appointments. The idea was to show off the talents of the repair crew on an instrument that displayed as many disparate styles as possible. Even the bridge pins were half black and half white. This guitar provided the seed of inspiration for the MTV-1 project.

East Indian rosewood, prized for its rich and warm effect on the bass resonance, was specified for the bass side of the guitar while mahogany, prized for its crisp and clear effect on the treble tones was chosen for the treble side. Oddly, each of these tonewoods is often criticized for lacking what the other possesses. The mixture of these woods seemed sensible, bold, and unprecedented, and the visual appearance fitted well with MTV's contemporary approach.

I worked extensively with Christopher A.D. in MTV's Off-Air Design Department. For every idea we accepted, a hundred were developed and discarded. The headstock art emerged with MTV's logo, inlaid in three shades of pearl, gold pearl and abalone. Larger "Unplugged" letters, stylized in MTV's bold "Ironmonger" font were inlaid in Paua shell inlay along the ebony fingerboard.

Eric Clapton stock model. After a rest of several years, MTV Unplugged 2.0 rose from the ashes with new acoustic performances from cutting-edge artists. We revived our collaboration with the MTV-2 Unplugged Edition, a 000 version of the original. This time, flamed maple was juxtaposed against the dark and beautiful coloration of East Indian rosewood to create an instrument of incredible contrast — both visually and tonally. The impact cannot be effectively judged at this point, but logic would suggest that new musical virtuosos will embrace the intimacy and purity of acoustic guitars. With any luck or foresight, Martin guitars will be right there to be embraced.

The MTV insignia in various shades of pearl takes a comfortable position in the cove of the Martin gold foil logo. Mixed mahogany and rosewood back and sides created a bold visual and tonal statement well-suited to MTV's cutting edge image.

JAPANESE EDITIONS

*Demanding specifications from two of Japan's most
cutting-edge acoustic guitar players*

AS A LOVER OF JAPANESE CULTURE with a particular affinity with sushi, I had the honor of traveling on Martin business to Japan for several dealer shows organized by Martin's Japanese distributor, T. Kurosawa & Co., Ltd. The extensive Martin Club of Japan presents acoustic concerts and special events that generally coincide with these. At one such show in May of 2000 I was privileged to hear several magnificent Japanese guitarists, among them Isato Nakagawa and Chuei Yoshikawa. Impressed with their virtuosity, I immediately began work on a series of specific artist signature editions.

Isato Nakagawa is one of Japan's most original, creative acoustic guitarists. He was a member of the legendary Japanese folk group Five Red Balloons. His mastery has helped to elevate the steel-string acoustic guitar in Japan to its rightful position as a respected solo instrument. Isato's percussive fingerstyle technique is distinctly original, yet his fresh songwriting draws inspiration from indigenous Japanese musical roots. Highly regarded by professional and amateur guitar players alike, Isato performs extensively throughout Japan, with a strong following in Europe.

The 000C-42 "1310" Signature Edition was fashioned after Isato's personal 14-fret 000-21 Martin that, like Eric Clapton's 000s, had been extensively customized in the 42 style. With a soundboard of Italian alpine spruce, the tone of these guitars is remarkably open and alive.

We based the design of Isato's signature edition on a full deck of playing cards, including two prototypes designated as "jokers." The edition was logically divided into four "suites" of thirteen spades, hearts, clubs, and diamonds. Each guitar was further designated as a specific playing card (Ace of Spades, Jack of Diamonds, etc.) An interior label, signed by Isato Nakagawa and Chris Martin, was placed adjacent to its actual designated playing card. The four "suites" of thirteen cards were further designated with a spade, heart, club, diamond, or joker inlay marking the 17th fret position.

Isato Nakagawa is known to carefully manicure the fingernails of his right hand to enhance his guitar technique. He cuts ovals from golden orange ping pong balls, superglues them on top of his existing nails, and

carefully files them to the perfect shape for fingerstyle playing. Hence, his nails are long and brilliantly colored which has, in effect, become his trademark. In Japanese, the number "1310" is pronounced "Is-a-to," a convenient numeric "signature" that is inlaid between the last fret in appropriately colored "ping-pong ball" orange composite material.

Like his good friend Isato, Chuei Yoshikawa is also regarded as one of Japan's most talented acoustic guitarists, producing and arranging many recordings and innumerable platinum hits over the past three decades. In his career as a soloist he has released seven albums to date. His virtuosity in the studio and onstage has had a significant and lasting impact upon Japanese music. He has produced many new Japanese artists, continued his extensive recording and touring schedule, and assumed the role of bandmaster on a popular Japanese television entertainment series.

Chuei was equally thrilled at the prospect of developing an artist edition. He had enjoyed playing one of the 00-16DB Women & Music models and immediately focused his signature-model design on a similar Dreadnought bodydepth 00-cutaway with mahogany back and sides and onboard electronics. The black ebony fingerboard is modestly understated, with simple diamonds and squares, and the unique silhouette of Chuei's eyeglasses with tiny pearl dots for eyes at the octave fret. Chuei's first name is inlaid with delicate simplicity at the last fret.

Chuei was particularly insistent on developing a sunburst pattern for his edition that was more reminiscent of vintage Gibson dark tobacco sunbursts. We worked hard to get the exact color combination he desired. The result was so clearly superior to any of Martin's previous sunburst attempts that Chuei's pattern started to appear on other Martin offerings and most likely will become a regular Martin option.

Though Isato and Chuei's models are very different, they serve the distinct needs of each performer ideally. These first two Japanese signature models will no doubt pave the way not only for future Japanese signature editions but also for artists significant to other international cultures.

This Page: One of two "joker" prototypes of the Isato Nakagawa 000C-42 "1310" Signature Edition. Right: Chuei Yoshikawa's 00-16DBCY Signature Edition was also offered with a cutaway option. Inset: Chuei Yoshikawa (top) and Isayo Nakagawa (bottom).

Like his good friend Isato, Chuei Yoshikawa is also regarded as one of Japan's most talented acoustic guitarists

According to their wishes, charitable proceeds from both the Isato Nakagawa and Chuei Yoshikawa signature edition guitars were donated in support of disaster relief for volcano victims on the Miyake, Ni, and Kozu Islands off of the east coast of Japan.

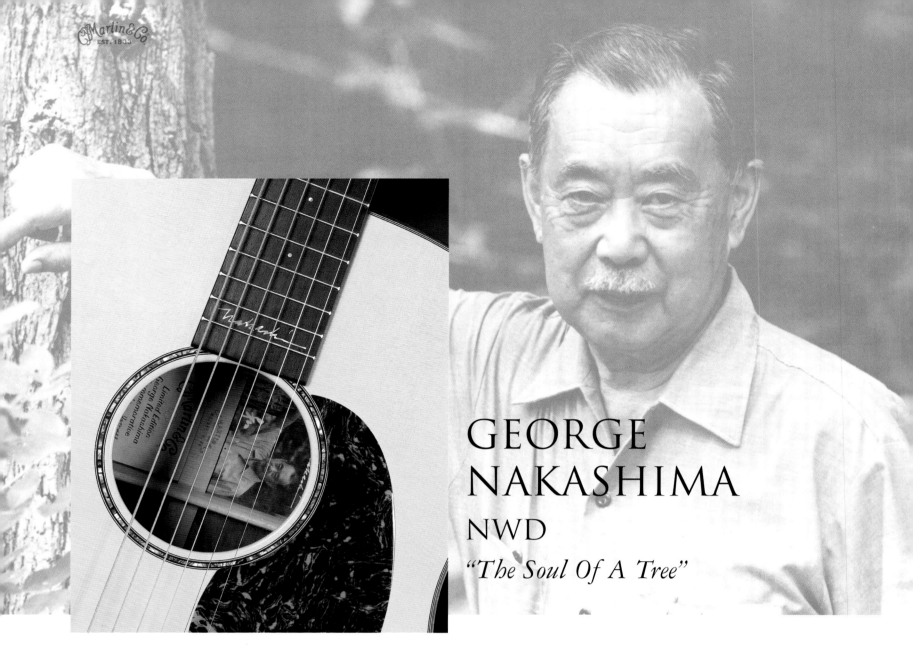

GEORGE NAKASHIMA
NWD
"The Soul Of A Tree"

IN THE EARLY 1970S, Martin's head of Research and Development, Dr. Don Thompson, endeavored to construct the Martin Sawmill. The idea was to achieve greater cost savings and control over quartersawing by importing East Indian rosewood logs. It was an ambitious plan. The only hitch was that very shortly after the mill was completed, the Indian government placed an embargo on the exportation of logs, thereby rendering Martin's million-dollar sawmill a white elephant. In an attempt to make the best of a difficult situation, the sawmill began importing and cutting other species of exotic woods for sale to the high-end woodworking market. Concurrently, Martin sought customers that might need precision custom cutting of their own logs.

George Nakashima's woodworking shop was conveniently located an hour south of Nazareth in the little town of New Hope, and since his extraordinary furniture designs depended upon the acquisition and precision cutting of rare oversized walnut logs, Martin's state-of-the-art bandmill was perfectly suited to George's needs. He soon became Martin's first and foremost custom cutting customer.

For those unfamiliar with Nakashima, his work is on display in many of the finest museums and homes around the world. Inspired by his love of Japanese fine craftsmanship and simplicity of design, his superb craftsmanship and use of organic materials soon earned him a lasting international reputation. He is widely heralded as the founding father of the contemporary American woodworking movement. George Nakashima died at age eighty-five in 1990, but his woodworking studio and artistic legacy are carried on to this day by his daughter, Mira Nakashima Yarnall.

We maintained our friendship and connection with Mira long after the Martin Sawmill ceased cutting logs. She was a tried-and-true Martin guitar owner and player. On one of Mira's visits, Chris Martin suggested the idea of co-designing a special commemorative guitar as a testimonial to the long and warm relationship between Martin and the Nakashima family. Mira was thrilled with the idea, and a

group of Martin employees soon traveled to New Hope to get a firsthand appreciation of the Nakashima style, scope, and legacy.

In keeping with the distinctive organic furniture style developed by Nakashima, rare highly figured Claro walnut, George's favorite wood species, was chosen for the sides and back. The back panels were uniquely joined with two of Nakashima's trademark dovetailed "butterflies" fashioned from East Indian rosewood. As ornamentation, the Nakashima family crest, a five-petal Japanese ivy leaf, was inlaid in pearl beneath Martin's script logo into a matching Claro walnut headplate. The delicate petals of the family crest were "disassembled" and used as fingerboard position markers, culminating with Nakashima's elegant signature in pearl at the last fret. With a soundboard of rare Italian alpine spruce, lightly aged with a soft toner and finished with satin lacquer, the guitar possessed an integrity of design that was in perfect congruity with Nakashima's spirit.

The instruments needed to be seen to be fully understood, but it didn't take long for the marketplace to realize how tonally, visually, and emotionally special the Nakashima guitars really were. All one hundred of the NWD editions sold soon after the first models appeared. The charitable proceeds were donated to The Nakashima Foundation For Peace, helping to fulfill George's dream of providing "altars of peace" for each of the seven continents on Earth. To date, magnificent Claro tables have been consecrated and installed at the Cathedral of St. John the Divine in New York City, at the Russian Academy of Art in Moscow, and at the "City of Peace" in Aurovoille, India. One hundred more portable "guitars of peace" enable George Nakashima's same urgent message to resonate around the world.

Above: George Nakashima respected wood and gave it new life in his organic designs. Inset: Top detail of the Nakashima NWD, showing Jack Rosen's photographic portrait from inside the soundhole. Right: The NWD guitar is in good company next to one of the elegant Nakashima "conoid" chairs.

122

EMPLOYEE TASK TEAM
EMP-1, EMP-2 & EMP-NS

From work place to show place

FOLLOWING CHRIS MARTIN'S INITIATIVE, several other task teams sprouted up at Martin. The employees in the Pearl Inlay Department were challenged directly by Chris Martin to design a guitar that would incorporate new pearl inlay materials and techniques. Several interesting prototypes emerged but there was no concensus for a single model, and so the ideas were either left to languish or be picked up by another task team.

The rather loosely defined Employee Guitar Group was successful in bringing three interesting models to the market, the EMP-1 Employee Edition being the most lucrative. With an ambitious and hopeful edition size of 262, the EMP-1 blended some fresh southwestern appointments with a contemporary cutaway body shape. The dealers liked the model because it appealed to younger

electric players "crossing over" to acoustic guitar and an impressive number of 232 guitars were sold.

The EMP-2 was not as successful, since bending difficulty with the certified T'zalam (pronounced Sal-am) guitar sides forced the model to be withheld prematurely and consequently only thirty instruments were completed.

The EMP-NS Employee Model was designed by a group of fervent and proud nightshift employees and inspired by the dark shadows of the evening. A smokey black Jacobean stain was applied atop a flamed maple back and sides to create a handsome instrument that netted a respectable seventy-three dealer orders.

Counterclockwise from Upper Right: The EMP-1 with a southwestern flair; the EMP-2 with certified T'zalam; and a detail of the EMP-NS with its black-stained maple-flamed back.

VETERANS TASK TEAM
DVM
A fervent commitment by employees to develop this unique tribute

A GOOD NUMBER OF MARTIN EMPLOYEES are military veterans or are at least closely related to someone who served in the armed forces. The tremendous pride felt by these co-workers led to the formation of a Veteran's Task Team that hoped to bring a Veteran's Guitar model to market. I agreed to sit in and help the group with inlay art and model specifications.

The group was rather large and many of the initial meetings produced ideas that were difficult to transform into viable or workable guitar designs. We tried to acquire military buttons from each of the armed services for insetting into the fingerboard, but we simply couldn't find a reliable supplier. Several eagle designs were considered for the headstock, but they were all either too detailed for inlay or not in the public domain. Cindy McAllister, head of Martin's MIS Department, was the group's most fervent and persistent member. She gradually assumed a leadership role and kept the group focused during quite a few frustrating setbacks.

Building upon Martin's popular herringbone Dreadnought as a base model, the elements began to fall into place. Cindy was successful in procuring the five military insignia lapel pins (Army, Navy, Marines, Air Force, and Coast Guard) that found a very appropriate and attractive position nested vertically under the Martin logo on the headstock. The fingerboard combined the letters of the word "VETERANS" with the simple but elegant eagle design borrowed from the Bicentennial D-76. The colorful service award for active military duty, beautifully recreated by Pearlworks in wood marquetry, found a perfect spot at the final fret. To top it off, we located a source for genuine dog tags that could be custom stamped with the serial number of each guitar in the edition.

Permission from each of the five branches of the armed forces needed to be secured in order to use the military insignias. Once again, the persistence of Cindy McAllister paid off. She enlisted the invaluable assistance of our local representative Pat Toomey, and one by one, the letters of approval came in.

The prototypes were very handsome and, to the group's delight, more than three hundred orders were placed for the "DVM" guitar at its Anaheim NAMM introduction in January of 2002. Ironically, the guitar was conceived more than a year in advance of the tragic events surrounding September 11, 2001, and as American troups headed off for Afghanistan (and subsequently Iraq), the guitar was an especially genuine and timely tribute. In keeping with the clear wishes of the team, the royalties from the sale of each guitar were donated in support of disabled veterans.

Top: A detail of the DVM soundhole reveals the service award for active military duty, inlaid in colorful marquetry at the final fret. Bottom: The DVM headstock serves as a perfectly appropriate backdrop for the five enameled insignias of the US armed forces.

SCOTT CHINERY GOLIATH
A giant guitar for a larger-than-life man

SCOTT CHINERY WAS ONE OF THE WORLD'S MOST significant collectors of musical instruments. Scott became a self-made millionaire by marketing the Cybergenics bodybuilding and weight-loss products. He sold his successful company and retired to a luxurious home in Tom's River, New Jersey where, with his wife Kathy, he raised four children and amassed a remarkable collection of acoustic, electric, and archtop guitars. Our tiny museum paled in comparison to Scott's selection of rare Martin instruments and eventually, Chris Martin and I traveled to Tom's River to have a sushi lunch at Scott's home and see what we'd heard so much about. We were both stunned at the depth and breadth of the collection and at Scott's passion for the instruments. I was particularly flattered that my special 7-42 "Dick Boak" custom guitar had ended up in Scott's hands.

Scott was also a collector of Batman memorabilia. He owned one of the original Batmobiles, plus Robin's Bat-cycle. As a connoisseur of rare cars, great food, fine wines, and premium cigars, he was very well versed in the good things of life. He was a warm, happy, intelligent, and cordial individual with a magnetic personality.

Chris was so impressed with the collection that he asked Scott whether a larger group from Martin might come out to visit. Scott graciously agreed and about twenty-five Martin staff members arrived for a remarkable in-depth look at the collection and an outstanding lunch of poached salmon.

Scott had a most unusual and rather gigantic Larson guitar with a body width of nearly nineteen inches. Being a man of great stature himself, it seemed understandable that Scott would take a particular liking to the large Larson. He wanted to commission an up-to-date version, but with Martin's attention to tonality, detail, and lightness of construction. We were excited about the project and returned to Nazareth with many ideas about how to approach such a large instrument. We dubbed the project The Chinery Goliath.

Dale Eckhart, Martin's prototype maker at that time, and Bill Hall, then manager of Support Services, enjoyed taking on the challenge. Dale fabricated a special adjustable mold that could accommodate the large body. Bill and I selected extra wide sets of Sitka spruce and East Indian rosewood. Even so, it was necessary to flip-flop excess wood from the upper bout down to the lower bout, making a four-piece bookmatch to achieve the extreme width. Extra long X-braces were laid into a traditional Martin super-X frame and adjusted to strengthen the top without jeopardizing the tone or risking a severe belly behind the bridge. Lastly, at Scott's request, a unique Style-45 headplate of Sitka spruce was inlaid with contrasting C. F. Martin block letters in ebony.

A prototype was assembled "in the white" (without finish) and strung up to pitch to test the strength of the neck and the deflection of the top under tension. There were several adjustments made to the internal structure, after which the actual model was initiated. The result was magnificent. A proud Scott Chinery showed up at the factory to pick up the finished instrument.

The annual Great American Guitar Show in King Of Prussia, Pennsylvania was the perfect venue to unveil the Chinery Goliath. In his usual style, Scott took a significant display space, trucked the Batmobile down to Philadelphia and hired Batman himself, Adam West, to come and sign autographs. George Gruhn had agreed to dress up in one of Scott's Batman costumes for a photo opportunity, but he was late. I showed up just in time to don the outfit and sit in the Batmobile with music media's Lisa Sharkin dressed as Batgirl for a magazine photo shoot. The Goliath stood nearby in a custom-made cherry display case where occasional gawkers and nimble guitarists were invited to take it down and sample the immense sound for themselves.

It seemed inconceivable when we heard the shocking news that Scott had died of heart failure at the young age of forty. His passing is a tremendous loss for so many people. The photographs of the Goliath and of Scott beaming with joy evoke strong memories of Scott Chinery, truly an irrepressible and life-loving character.

Above left: A rear view of the Goliath. Right: In Scott Chinery's capable hands, this magnificent guitar seemed quite normal in size. Opposite Page: Goliath top detail.

CEO'S CHOICE
Enhancing the heritage with fresh new ideas

CHRIS MARTIN HAS SOME VERY DEFINITE IDEAS ABOUT GUITAR DESIGN and has always enjoyed the process of bringing new ideas to the market. As the Chief Executive Officer of the company, he takes a very proactive stand in favor of progress and manufacturing efficiency. At the same time it is his clear responsibility to protect the incredible heritage that his family has passed on to him.

In 1997 he had an idea to produce a pair of personal signature models for which he would choose all the specifications. His initial criteria, though never elaborated in writing, dealt with tonality, aesthetics, new processes, use of technology, and value for the customer.

The mahogany CEO-1 and the rosewood CEO-1R were straightforward Dreadnoughts, enhanced with many of Chris's favorite appointments, including a very classy vintage-styled tweed case. The most striking visual aspect of the guitars were the hollow hexagon inlays, a feature that Chris championed from its inception in the early eighties, and his favorite binding configuration — N-20-style black bindings with simple black/white top, back, and side inlay. The models were very affordable, they sounded great, they were loaded with features generally found on much higher-priced models, and with combined sales in excess of 300 instruments they were clearly successful.

Chris continued to focus his efforts on optimum aesthetics, tone, and value with the CEO-2. This model was a collaboration with Steinway, who had sourced some very beautiful striped Macassar ebony veneer for their piano cases. After the large laminates were laid out and trimmed to the piano shape, there were invariably leftover sections large enough to reclaim some beautiful guitar sets. Accordingly, a handsome guitar was designed around this special wood incorporating many of the pre-defined appointments from the CEO-1 and CEO-1R models.

With the acquisition of some lovely Brazilian rosewood veneered laminates for back and sides, the CEO-3 once again took advantage of Chris's pre-established formula for appointments with a slight shift away from black, especially in the application of metallic gold lacquer to the soundboard, reminiscent of the gold top electrics made by a very large electric-guitar company that probably deserves introduction but will not get one here.

It is highly likely that Chris found great satisfaction, and perhaps some humor, in borrowing a feature such as the gold top from one of the competitors. After all, everyone on the block had borrowed heavily from Martin's designs throughout the years without any remuneration or feeling of remorse. Many of these annoyances are ancient history by now, but Chris used

Below: The CEO-1R blended Chris Martin's favorite specifications in a coherent and affordable package.
Right: The CEO-2 model utilized Steinway's striped-ebony laminates. Below Right: Chris's original CEO-1.

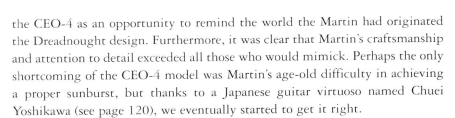

the CEO-4 as an opportunity to remind the world the Martin had originated the Dreadnought design. Furthermore, it was clear that Martin's craftsmanship and attention to detail exceeded all those who would mimick. Perhaps the only shortcoming of the CEO-4 model was Martin's age-old difficulty in achieving a proper sunburst, but thanks to a Japanese guitar virtuoso named Chuei Yoshikawa (see page 120), we eventually started to get it right.

The CEO-4 was so well received that a CEO-4R model with East Indian rosewood back and sides was added to the list, but this addition actually followed the introduction of the CEO-5 model — an instrument that through natural evolution returned to Martin's original 12-fret "standard" Dreadnought roots.

Chris had participated in a number of online forums and decided to invite the participants of these chat groups to send in their ideas for the optimum acoustic Martin guitar. Many ideas were submitted, leaving Chris with the dilemma of how to evaluate fairly or apply the ideas in each design. He came to the logical conclusion that, as the man in charge, it was his "choice." He went through all of the ideas diligently, selecting heavily bear-clawed spruce from one, herringbone pearl from another, environmentally friendly sapele from yet another, and so on until a model was gradually conceived from the ground up — an interesting amalgamation and approach that produced a series of remarkably gorgeous instruments.

Given the ongoing success of Chris's "CEO's Choice" editions, it is likely that he will continue to conjure instruments up from the depths of his subconscious and push the envelope in the process. That's his style, but remember that it has also been his style to insure that highly traditional Vintage Series and Golden Era recreations from Martin's finest moments be brought forward and preserved in the line. These two seemingly opposing initiatives constitute Chris's greatest and deserved legacy. We should all balance the past and the future with such style and grace.

COMMEMORATIVE EDITIONS
Looking back to the Founder for new inspiration

CHRISTIAN FREDERICK MARTIN was born in Markneukirchen, Germany on January 31, 1796. His story is certainly well known. He mastered the art of guitarmaking as foreman of Johann Stauffer's guitar factory in Vienna. After returning to his hometown to set up shop, the local Violin Maker's Guild objected and the dispute that ensued led to his family's emigration to America in 1833. Thriving in the New World, he eventually moved his home and business from New York to Nazareth in 1839. His son C. F. Martin Jr. carried on the family tradition, as did his grandson Frank Henry Martin. The flourishing operation survived the Civil War, the Spanish American War, World War I, and the Great Depression. Then there was C. F. Martin III and his son Frank Herbert. The company forged on through World War II, experiencing great success in the postwar era. During the tenure of Frank Herbert Martin, it was a time of acquisition and a new modern plant was built to accommodate the guitar boom of the sixties. The economy, however, began to falter. Crippled by a strike, the company nearly collapsed in the early eighties, but under the direction of a young C. F. Martin IV, the company got back on track with a new energy and open mindedness. Now Martin has experienced unprecedented growth and prosperity. It is amazing what C. F. Martin Sr. had initiated.

More than one hundred and sixty years later, Chris Martin sat in his office not far from the original Cherry Hill homestead, trying to think of appropriate ways to commemorate the founder's contribution to the development of the guitar. The Dreadnought guitar had played such an integral role in the success of the company that Chris decided to issue two D-45 Deluxe Limited Editions, one in Brazilian rosewood and one in East Indian rosewood, commemorating the 200th anniversary of his great great great grandfather's birth. The Deluxe style enhances the already ornate abalone-pearl bordering with the

addition of abalone trim at virtually every possible seam. Christian F. Martin Sr.'s quill-pen signature was carefully prepared for the inlay and positioned at the last fret of each edition guitar.

The two editions were well received. Retailing for a tidy sum of $19,500, all ninety-one of the Brazilian rosewood edition guitars sold quickly and 114 of the more affordable East Indian edition were constructed and delivered.

The success inspired Chris to continue the commemoration in 1997 with the introduction of two Martin "Stauffer" Limited Edition guitars. These were the first "Stauffer" models to be offered for sale since the mid 1800s, when C. F. Martin Sr. abandoned the asymmetrical shape in favor of the now-legendary Martin "square" headstock.

The Martin "Stauffer" Limited Edition 00-40 and 00-45 models paid tribute to the 12-fret guitars made during the very early years of the company. These graceful instruments had an unusual-shaped headstock with all tuning keys on one side, a feature borrowed from his mentor Johann Stauffer. When Leo Fender designed his initial electric guitars more than a century later, he borrowed this same headstock shape from Martin. The unusual headstock required that equally unusual tuning machines be developed with variable length posts. The guitars were quite noteworthy and helped to invigorate the appreciation and demand for traditional 12-fret Martin models.

Perhaps the most distinctive element of the project was an elegant accessory — a beautifully crafted recreation of Martin's original wooden "coffin" case, complete with mauve velvet interior and a replica parchment case label denoting size and style.

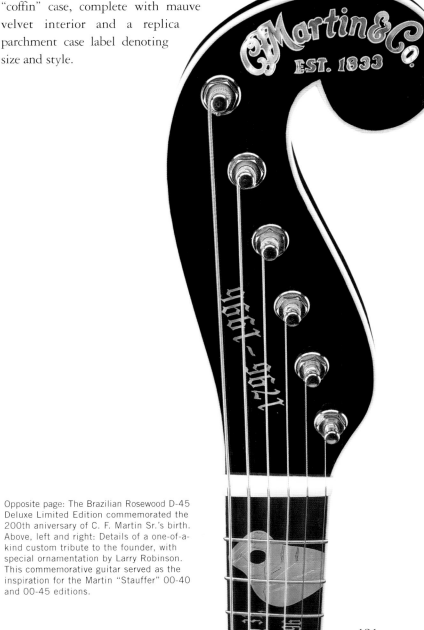

Opposite page: The Brazilian Rosewood D-45 Deluxe Limited Edition commemorated the 200th aniversary of C. F. Martin Sr.'s birth. Above, left and right: Details of a one-of-a-kind custom tribute to the founder, with special ornamentation by Larry Robinson. This commemorative guitar served as the inspiration for the Martin "Stauffer" 00-40 and 00-45 editions.

Opposite Page and Top Right: The 00-45S 1902 Limited Edition. Below Left: The original favorite of Roy Rogers, the OM-45 Delux Edition was limited to just fourteen special guitars.

00-45S 1902
Museum pieces brought back to life

IT WASN'T UNUSUAL FOR MARTIN to receive special-order requests for instruments with ornamentation that exceeded the 42 styling that was at the time Martin's top-of-the-line. Pearlwork on bowl-back mandolins of the era was often extremely lavish and, for several 1902 00-sized prototypes, some of that patterning was borrowed. These highly decorative floral vine inlays were expanded and refashioned into what we now refer to as the "Tree of Life" fingerboard pattern. A few different headplate inlay patterns were tested as well, two of which were variations of what is now called the Martin torch pattern, while a third came to be known as the "flowerpot" headstock pattern. Another feature borrowed from the mandolins was the equally ornate on-center scratchplate (or pickguard), located between the soundhole and the bridge.

While at least one of these 00 prototypes was fitted with standard Style-42 abalone trim, others were made with extra pearl bordering for the body binding of the side and back — a configuration that was eventually added to the Martin line in 1904 under a new Style-45 designation.

In the sixties, Martin employees Mike Longworth and Lester Wagner pooled their funds and purchased privately one of the 1902 prototypes with Style-45 ornamentation. A second 1902 prototype with Style-42 ornamentation had been similarly acquired by their co-worker Lester Davidson. When these two similar instruments were compared, it was discovered that they had identical serial numbers — an oddity that was most probably a shop error during manual stamping of the serial-number blocks.

In January of 2002, Martin issued a limited-edition recreation of the special 00-45S "1902," complete with replica coffin case. The special guitars were offered with rare pre-CITES Brazilian rosewood back and sides, 12-fret 00 body, and a tortoise-colored pickguard inlaid on center into the Adirondack spruce soundboard, a tree of life fingerboard, and a flowerpot inlaid into a traditional slotted headstock. The edition size was limited to no more than one hundred instruments.

OM-45 DELUXE
The crown jewel of the OMs

PRIOR TO THE 2001 UNVEILING of Martin's unprecedented D-50, the "OM-45 Deluxe" was the highest grade and most ornately styled Martin instrument ever cataloged. Only fourteen of these guitars were originally made, all in 1930. These were mostly offered by Sherman Clay's, a music store in San Francisco, and by Southern California Music in Los Angeles. One of the most prominent guitar players of the era, Leonard Slye (Roy Rogers) purchased one of these special guitars early in his career while still a member of the Sons of the Pioneers.

Similar in appointments to the OM-45, the OM-45 Deluxe had extra ornamentation: two abalone snowflakes on the bridge, and a floral pattern on the pickguard. In addition, the headstock was fitted with hand-engraved, gold-plated, banjo-style tuners with solid-pearl buttons.

In a more general sense, the Martin OM or "Orchestra Model" was the first truly modern flat-top guitar. The joining of a 25.4-inch long-scale neck with a small "000" body made it an extremely responsive and playable guitar. The treble tones are glassine and brilliant, and unlike many larger instruments, the bass is deep and clear without dominating the sound. As a solo, ensemble, or recording instrument, the OM remains highly sought-after by players of diverse styles.

The OM neck shape too has become a critical specification for most fingerstyle players. The slightly wider 1.75-inch width is still fast and comfortable and the wider string spacing allows plenty of room for complex fingerstyle chordings.

The OM-45GE Deluxe Limited Edition Golden Era model, introduced in 1998, was inspired by the original 1930 model. In keeping with the original quantity, the edition was limited to only fourteen instruments, each retailing for $27,500.

D-50 DELUXE FIRST EDITION

A shimmering masterpiece with unprecedented inlay

CHRIS MARTIN'S PURSUIT OF HIGHER END ultra-deluxe models was somewhat hindered by the difficulty in replicating extremely ornate inlays like those one-of-a-kind collaborative projects with Larry Robinson, or the occasional customer-driven inlay masterpieces by David Nichols of Custom Pearl Inlay, built in conjunction with the Martin Custom Shop.

On a fishing trip in the Chesapeake Bay with Larry Sifel and Jeff Harding of Pearlworks, Chris Martin initiated early discussions about his vision for a D-50 guitar. This would be a new top-of-the-line Martin style, significantly more ornate than the D-45. The biggest challenge of the project was to produce inlays that would take advantage of the capabilities, technologies, and techniques that Pearlworks had developed with their miniature CNC milling machines. Martin's traditional "Tree Of Life" pattern was chosen as the basis upon which to build a new design. The programming time would be tedious but the resulting patterns would be beyond compare.

The D-50 was the first Martin guitar to feature inlay on the instrument's sides and back. Two pairs of floral designs were planned for both sides of the back inlay strip, and for either side of the neck heel and end piece. These areas are typically flat — a good thing given that premium Brazilian rosewood sides would need to be bent and assembled after the inlays were set in place.

Tim Teel in Martin's R&D Department facilitated the project on the Martin side. Testing on the first prototype proved that these new ideas would actually work. We decided to limit the first D-50 edition to just fifty instruments, each individually numbered in sequence and signed by Chris Martin.

Every leaf, flower, and stem of the "Tree Of Life" was cut from highly colorful dark-heart abalone, then bordered with a thin band of mother-of-pearl creating a shimmering, almost jewel-like effect against the black ebony background.

Bound in grained ivoroid, Style-45 Deluxe abalone inlays were set at virtually every possible seam. Vintage-style gold Waverly tuning machines were individually hand-engraved. Fossil ivory was specified for the nut, saddle, and pins of the bridge, which were further enhanced with star-sapphire inlays and 14-karat gold settings. A special 5-ply hardshell case trimmed with genuine top-hide leather, lined with crushed burgundy velvet, and equipped with an onboard humidity and temperature gauge, was furnished with each instrument.

With respect to tonewoods, the sides, back, headplate, end piece and heel cap were all crafted with Martin's highest grade of CITES Certified Brazilian rosewood. Soundboards were bookmatched from premium-grade Sitka spruce with heavy "bearclaw" figuring. Labor and materials for the unprecedented inlay work priced the guitars well above $60,000. Chris Martin, nevertheless, felt it was imperative that the model retail at no more than $50,000. We had no idea whether we would sell even a single guitar, though everyone that saw the prototype thought it to be absolutely stunning. We were of course elated — not to say startled — when all fifty guitars in the edition sold within days of their introduction at the January 2001 NAMM Show in Anaheim.

Actually making the guitars proved to be a further challenge. It took the better part of two years before all of the instruments passed through

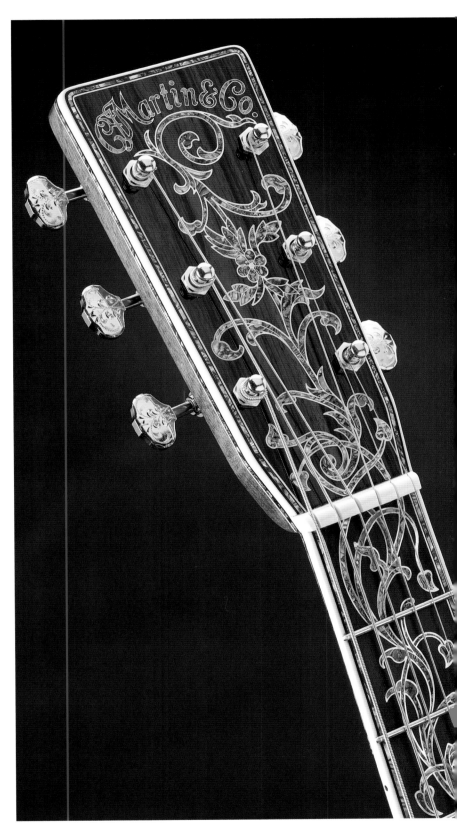

the painstaking pearl-inlay process. Hopefully the instruments will be played on occasion; they deserve nothing less given the uncompromised nature of the finest tonal materials, but we suspect that these instruments may likely rise above the rigours of everyday usage to stand as works of art — the highest representatives of the guitarmaking craft — worthy of display in museums or private collections.

Opposite Page: The exquisite detailing of the D-50 included herringbone pearl body trim plus abalone inlays bordered in mother-of-pearl on the fingerboard, pickguard, headplate, and other positions too numerous to mention. Above: The D-50 headstock detail showing deluxe pearl trim and hand-engraved gold tuning machines.

LARRY ROBINSON

Collaborations with an inlay master

LARRY ROBINSON IS AN INLAY ARTIST who resides in Sonoma County, California. He began cutting inlays in 1975 while working for Alembic, the guitar company that built many of the instruments used by Haight-Ashbury rock bands of the mid-sixties including, but not limited to, The Grateful Dead, Fleetwood Mac, Jefferson Airplane, The Who, and Led Zeppelin. Larry's proficiency quickly evolved and he is now considered one of the finest inlay artists alive today.

Inlay of this variety is typically glued into a cavity that has been excavated from the surface. The actual inlay is usually scroll-cut by hand with a jeweler's saw, then set into place with superglue or epoxy resin and sanded flush. Few inlay artists stray from the traditional choices, mother-of-pearl and abalone shell being the most common. Larry augments his color palette with a seemingly endless array of silver, gold, copper, brass, bone, tusk, wood veneer, composite stone, turquoise, and anything else that suits his need for a specific inlay motif. Unlike inlay designs programmed on the CNC for instrument production, Larry avoids such technology, opting instead to focus on unique one-of-a-kind hand-cut art pieces, for which the more tedious computer work is simply not cost effective.

Larry rebuffs compliments about his artistic talent explaining that he borrows inspiration from a large library of graphic resources. While this may be true, his ability to compose and assimilate a multitude of images into a cohesive and inspired design is in itself a true art form. He is clearly a master of that skill and his technical execution is flawless.

Above Left: Larry Robinson at work in his California studio cutting the soundhole "rose" for Martin Serial #1,000,000 due to be completed in 2004. Right: The Brazilian rosewood Art Nouveau D-45 was one of the early design collaborations with inlay artist Larry Robinson.

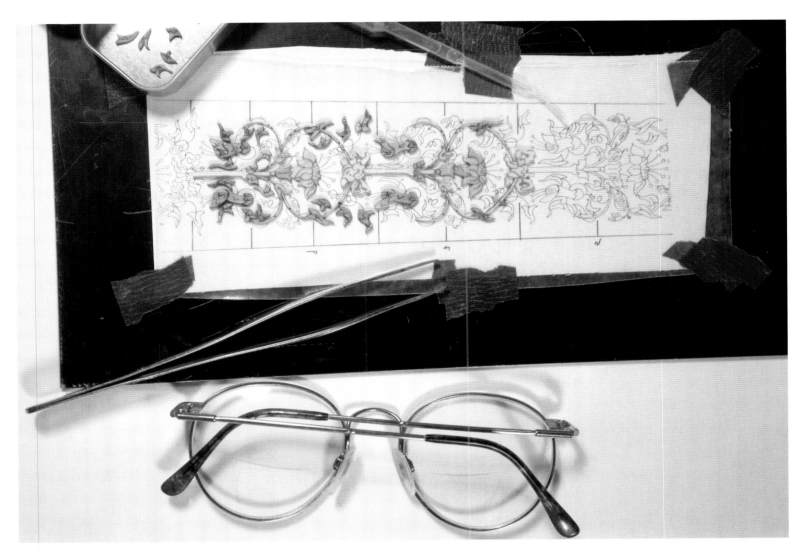

Above: Using the actual size design drawing of the inlay pattern, Larry Robinson begins to organize the myriad of hand-cut components that will become the extraordinary fingerboard of the #1,000,000 guitar.

Somewhere along the line, Chris Martin learned about or met up with Larry. Neither can remember the exact occasion. It was most likely one of the guitarmaking symposiums that I had organized while acting as Executive Director of The Association Of Stringed Instrument Artisans (ASIA). In any event, Chris came away with one of Larry's books and was immensely impressed with his inlay talent. After several follow-up phone calls, Chris commissioned Larry to design and execute the head-stock and fingerboard inlays for a special one-of-a-kind Stauffer (see page 129) model to commemorate the impending 200th birthday anniversary of the company founder, C. F. Martin Sr.

Larry gleaned the images from various Martin publications: a portrait of Christian Frederick from the earliest days of photography, a line drawing of the old factory that C. F. Sr. built next to the Martin homestead on North Street, a photograph of Martin's influential X-bracing pattern and the equally groundbreaking Dreadnought body shape. The completed inlays found their place on Martin Custom Serial #566578. The result was spectacular, exceeding Chris Martin's highest expectations. The guitar provided inspiration for the subsequent 1997 00-40 and 00-45 Limited Edition Stauffer Commemorative guitars. More importantly, this first collaboration with Larry Robinson set the stage for several further projects, each one reaching to out-do its predecessor.

Following the Stauffer commemorative, Chris's and Larry's discussions focused on a Brazilian rosewood D-45 with an inlay motif that drew its inspiration from turn-of-the-century art-nouveau design. It was agreed that the woods selected for the instrument would be absolutely premium; in fact they were hand-selected by Chris Martin himself from personal stock that was being saved for special projects of this nature. The soundboard was bookmatched from Adirondack red spruce, highly prized for its clarity of tone. The fingerboard, headplate, pickguard, bridge, heel cap, and endpiece were all pre-dimensioned and sent over to Larry Robinson's shop.

Over the course of the several months that followed, Larry immersed himself in the meticulous art-nouveau inlay motif. He created a headplate inlay with the C. F. Martin script logo in abalone bordered in mother-of-pearl, and the fingerboard inlays flowed with a natural liquidity reminiscent of Alphonse Mucha's organic style. Upon completion, Larry shipped the parts back to Nazareth.

Concurrently, luthier Jim Triggs hand-carved the neck heel in a traditional floral style. The guitar was then carefully assembled. Gold-plated tuning machines received special buttons embossed with a decorative Martin "M." Style-45 Deluxe inlay, selected from highly colorful abalone shell, was added to the seams of the neck and body and after final lacquering, Serial #581723 was completed and proudly displayed at every opportunity.

With Serial #600,000 quickly approaching, Chris and Larry continued their conversations. An important precedent had been set with the making of Martin Serial #500,000: as the half-millionth Martin guitar made, Chris wished to make it special. A stock-model Herringbone HD-28 was built and the spruce soundboard was meticulously signed prior to lacquering by nearly 300 Martin employees on the payroll at that time. The instrument became part of the company's extensive collection and is generally on display at the Martin Museum.

There was no question, however, that the collaborations with Larry Robinson that followed had exceeded and perhaps overshadowed the simplicity of Serial #500,000. For such a significant company milestone as Serial #600,000, Chris wished to do something even more lavish and Larry provided some initial sketches of traditional Celtic design that seemed to fit the bill.

Again Chris felt comfortable with the selection of Martin's flagship Dreadnought shape as the vehicle upon which to add Style-45 Deluxe embellishment, and once again Brazilian rosewood was selected from private stock and combined with Italian alpine spruce;

the same species used by Antonio Stradivarius for his prized violins. The headplate employed the traditional Martin D-45 letters that were rendered in a classic Celtic form. The finalized inlays for the fingerboard, bridge, pickguard, endpiece, and heel cap were composed with bits of imagery from various Celtic sourcebooks. As Larry often reiterates, the key to this type of work is in the arrangement — everything needs to work well together in a unified theme and coherent design.

The Celtic guitar and the art-nouveau model make a handsome pair. The degree of inlay on each instrument is equally impressive and with their premium tonewoods, they are indeed very special. Chris perceived these guitars as great showpieces and as genuine inspiration for Custom Shop clientele. A photoshoot combined these two models with a third Custom D-41 cutaway for the cover of Martin's Custom Shop catalog, after which the guitars traveled, often as a pair, to various trade shows and festivals. Instruments with such high value invariably intimidate guitarists, but Chris has always encouraged players to pick them up and try them — carefully, of course.

Chris continued to commission milestone projects with Larry Robinson. Often working through Custom Shop manager Bob Fehr, Larry was encouraged to submit increasingly more ornate design proposals for Chris's scrutiny and approval. For Serial #700,000, a pan-Asian theme was conceived that combines predominantly Chinese design motifs with Japanese and Buddhist elements. Through the early stages of its fabrication, the guitar was referred to as The China Guitar, but as the evolving designs were diversified the model was dubbed The D-45 Dragon.

There were so many concurrent and hidden themes buried within the inlays that we were dependent upon Larry to provide us with an explanatory text to accompany the guitar. That text, which follows in Larry's own words, is perhaps as exotic as the inlays described:

"The image in the central and lower area of the peghead is a 'hi' or 'pi' disc, usually made of jade and often found in tombs of Han Dynasty Emperors. They were symbols of Heaven and often had the double dragon motif. The borders and dots on the disc were raised above the surface. This inlay is 18k gold with sea snail accents and a bit of mother-of-pearl. The cloud and diamond border is a fairly common Chinese design, often found on furniture. The Martin logo is an 18k gold

frame enclosing green abalone. Note that the periods after 'Co.' and 'Est.' are also gold circles around dots of shell, and that everything was hand-cut, not CAD or Pantograph produced.

The fingerboard drawing was manipulated somewhat to fit on a tapered area and bend around the bottom. The original image is a painting on a leather-covered box from about the 1st Century B.C. Again we see the dragon motif, which at that time was already considered a spiritual animal. This is reminiscent of Celtic artwork but predates it by hundreds of years. Materials in the fingerboard are 18k gold framework, surrounding green abalone heart pieces. The dragonheads are black mother-of-pearl from Tahiti.

The dragon on the pickguard is similar to an inlay in an eight-lobed tray from the 14th Century that is now displayed in a Tokyo Museum. The original dragon is about 10 inches tall, has over 1,800 separate pieces of shell, and faces the other way. This one is too small to cut the scales individually, so I didn't even bother to draw them in, but I used some blue paua heart that looks just like small scales. It has five toes on each foot, so it probably belonged to someone in a royal family. Other parts of the dragon are cut from sea snail, gold, and red abalone. The clouds are typical representations of Chinese artwork and were taken from a book on paper cutting. They are 14k gold outlines with sea snail interiors. Again, the border is a fairly standard Chinese design, and was made by alternating gold and platinum.

The flowers on the bridge wings were found in some paintings, and the inlay behind the bridge pin holes is derived from a wall sculpture in the Forbidden City in Peking. The flowers are mother-of-pearl with gold accents, and the other bridge inlay is 18k gold with green abalone and sea snail details.

The two inlays on the tail pin (end piece) strip are Buddhist vajra, symbols of deep awareness and mental clarity. They were among the few images I found that were already inlays. They were done in pearl, or maybe snail, as part of the bordering on a pedestal for a statue of Buddha. These two are gold, ivory, and shell.

The calligraphy on the heel cap translates to 'harmony,' specifically the musical kind. It too is 18k gold sheet."

In early January of 2000, Chris Martin and Larry Robinson began a discussion about an inlay design for Martin's 750,000th guitar. Chris urged Larry to really push the limits and he certainly did — the initial design drawings represented such a detailed and vast project that Chris felt it necessary to reign in Larry's creativity and subsequently his price.

Larry suggested that the inlay motif reflect the origins of the instrument in the Middle East, and evoke an aura of seventeenth-century instruments that were built for members of royal families. The original, more ornate design included inlays up the center of the sides and back of the neck, cast-sculpted gold-tuning machine buttons, emeralds in all of the peacock feathers and gold Arabic calligraphy everywhere, but due to time constraints and untried manufacturing techniques, Larry focused his inlay efforts on the D-45 Peacock illustrated. In spite of its scaled-down design, the guitar took more than a year to complete.

The border around the back, sides, pick-guard, and neck is comprised of over two

Left: The D-45 Peacock commemorates the milestone of Martin Serial #750,000. At the time of its construction, this guitar was the most ornate Martin instrument ever constructed, surpassed only by the making of Serial #1,000,000, in process as this book approaches publication, and slated for potential completion and unveiling at the Winter NAMM Show in January of 2004. Right: The detail of the end pieces and side inlay reveal literaly thousands of hand-cut decorative inlay. Opposite Page: A magnificent peacock graces the back of Serial #750,000.

thousand hand-cut pieces of shell. The only pieces that weren't cut by hand are the small shell dots. On the neck are two elaborate peacocks with a silhouette of trees and bushes in 22-karat gold wire. The peacock on the peghead has a large plate of engraved gold for the feathers and the Martin logo is outlined in gold as well. On the bridge wings are two cast-gold medallions with marquis diamonds that reflect sections of the pattern on the pickguard. Behind the bridge pin row is a delicate floral arrangement with small diamonds in the flowers. Inside the shell-inlaid rosette is a removable sound-hole screen reminiscent of traditional lute rosette designs. Finally emerging from a Moorish arch composed of several varieties of Corian® is an exquisite peacock inlaid into a back of rare Brazilian rosewood. The peacock is composed primarily of green abalone, paua shell, and mother-of-pearl. The body of the peacock is estate ivory with a carefully set diamond for an eye.

A special revolving stand was fabricated for the Peacock guitar so that both the front and the back could be seen by a crowd of onlookers, but the stand was abandoned because of the all-too-real risk of toppling.

At the time of its construction and during the writing of this book, the D-45 Peacock guitar is the most ornate Martin instrument ever crafted. Appraised at more than $350,000, Martin has turned down several purchase offers at or above the appraised value. The instrument is part of Martin's permanent collection and is on display in a specially fabricated glass-backed case in the Martin Museum.

If and when The Peacock is surpassed, it will most certainly be the next Martin collaboration with Larry Robinson that does it. Initial design work for Serial #1,000,000 began early in 2002. The guitar will combine a multitude of Baroque and Victorian imagery. Larry explains that the styles are so similar that most people wouldn't be able to differentiate them anyway.

In addition to the unprecedented inlay work on Serial #1,000,000, there will be a significant amount of metal engraving that will be executed by world-class engraver Dave Giulietti. Dave will also be fabricating special medallions for the bridge wings and creating tube settings for all the jewels.

With a working title of #1M, Serial #1,000,000 is scheduled for completion in 2004. Like the Martin and Larry Robinson collaborations that have preceded it, a new pinnacle of guitarmaking craft and ornamentation will be reached. Then the question will surely be raised "What could possibly come next?"

THE FUTURE

One in a million

WHAT WILL THE FUTURE ADD TO THE INCREDIBLE legacy of C. F. Martin & Co.? Surely the inertia and infrastructure of the company is perfectly poised to continue for decades if not centuries to come.

In spite of the fact that supplies of traditional guitarmaking tonewoods will become more expensive and difficult to acquire during this new century, Martin will continue to offer high end solid wood guitars — after all, Martin seems to be one of the only companies with the right combination of design and craftsmanship to do justice to such special materials. Solid-wood instruments should continue to accrue in value, just as the instruments of the prewar era have proven, for the most part, to be excellent tonal and financial investments.

The market for alternatives to traditional tonewoods will also continue to develop quickly, probably out of sheer necessity. Some of these alternatives are already succeeding in giving traditional tonewoods a run for their money. And with new materials, new processes will evolve. That's good business and it will ultimately benefit the consumer.

It took Martin nearly 160 years to produce the first 500,000 instruments, yet it will take less than fourteen years (very soon to be accomplished) to produce the second 500,000 guitars. Tremendous growth has occurred at C. F. Martin & Co. in the past several decades. In 1964, Martin production moved from the old North Street plant to the more modern Sycamore Street facility and the new building has been repeatedly expanded upon to what is now more than twice its original size. In the same amount of time, the number of employees has grown from a little more than one hundred all the way up to seven hundred. With such dramatic development there are bound to be some growing pains, but the remarkable fact remains that Martin is producing some of the finest guitars made in the history of the company — so much so that many reverently refer to this current time period as the Martin's Guitar Company's second Golden Era.

It is certain that Martin guitars possess an intangible magic. It is the result of a singularly inspired yet evolutionary design, a Pennsylvania-German culture of precision craftsmanship with exceptionally high expectations and attention to detail, a consistent commitment to the utilization of the finest materials available, all working with an energy spurred by the genius of the founder carefully nurtured by six generations of Martin family members and their loyal employees.

That magic is a fragile treasure, currently balanced delicately between a web of old-world craftsmanship and precision technology. It is our job to insure that the magic is not lost so that future generations can enjoy what we have enjoyed. As George Nakashima once explained, a tree has a soul. When we cut one down we have an opportunity and an obligation to extract something that extols the incredible majesty of the tree.

What better eulogy
     for the tree and the wood
than a great guitar,
    one that sings, one that responds
  in the hands
     of a passionate player.

    One that is a Martin!

Opposite Page: A pickguard inlay detail showing Martin's X-bracing innovation; the vertex of the pickguard depicting tools of the luthier's trade.

ARTIST INDEX
Page numbers in bold indicate a signature edition

ALL GUITAR PHOTOGRAPHY BY JOHN STERLING RUTH UNLESS OTHERWISE CREDITED.

PICTURE CREDITS 6 Photo by Kim Miller; 8 Photo by Shawn Kelley; 12 Guitar appears courtesy of Ed Britt; 14 (bottom) Photo courtesy of Pat Terry, Jr., International Banjo magazine; 17 Photo courtesy of Autry Qualified Interest Trust; 20 (top) Photo by John Bellisimo; 21 (top left) Photo by Ron Keith; 22 Guitar appears courtesy of Travis Tritt; 23 (bottom) Guitar appears courtesy of Travis Tritt; 24 Photo by Doug Berry; 26 Photo by Christian Weber; 27 (left) Photo by Shawn Kelley; 28 Photo by Derek Berron; 29 Illustration courtesy of Ernest Tubb Record Shops, Nashville, Tennessee; 31 (top) Guitar appears courtesy of Minnie Snow and Jimmie Rodgers Snow; 32 Photo by Piper Ferguson; 35 Tim Jones Photography, Nashville, Estate of Hank Williams, Sr. by CMG Worldwide, Inc., courtesy PolyGram Records; 36 Photo courtesy of Kitty Wells and the Country Music Foundation archives; 39 Original Lester Flatt D-28 appears courtesy of Marty Stuart; 39 (background) Photo courtesy of Marty Stuart; 40 (right) Photo courtesy of Keith Case & Associates; 42 (top) Photo by Alan L. Mayor (www.wireimage.com); 43 Image courtesy of Gaylord Entertainment; 44 (right) Photo courtesy of Gaylord Entertainment; 46 (background) Elvis and Elvis Presley are registered trademarks with the USPTO, (inset) Martin Archives; 48 (left) Photo by Bill Bush; 50 Photo courtesy of Bob Shane, The Kingston Trio; 51 Guitar appears courtesy of Joan Baez; 53 Photo by Fred Solomacha; 54 Acoustic Guitar magazine cover courtesy of String Letter Press; 56 Photo courtesy of The Woody Guthrie Archives; 57 (bottom) Photo courtesy of Preston Gratoit; 58 Photo courtesy of Mark Moss, Sing Out! Magazine; 61 Photo B. Spremo/Toronto Star, courtesy of Mike Seeger; 62 (bottom) Photo by Dick Boak; 63 Photo by Dick Boak; 66 Photo by Gayle Burns, courtesy of Judy Collins; 72 Photo by Robert Knight; 71 (top) Photo by Doug Berry; 75 (top) Photo www.wireimage.com; 77 (background) Photo courtesy of Dan Fogelberg & HK Management; 83 (middle) Photo by Ray Stanyard; 85 (left) Photo by John Sterling Ruth; 86 (left) Photo by Dick Boak; 91 Photo by Sherri Rayn Barnett; 93 Photo courtesy of Sharon & Peter Donegan; 96 Photo by Gered Mankowitz; 97 Photo by Max Goldstein, Star File, Inc.; 101 Photo by Juta Sugai; 103 (bottom) Photo by Roy Kidney; 104 Photo courtesy of the International Guitar Research Archives; 105 (bottom) Photo courtesy of Diane Ponzio, photo by Sardi Klein; 107 (center) Photo courtesy of Shawn Colvin, Lisa Arzt and AGF Entertainment; 110 (top) Photo by Sam Ericson; 111 (top) Photo by Charlie Gross; 112 (background) Photo by Mike Sanders; 113 (top) Photo by Mike Savoia – www.sugarray.com; 114 (top) Photo by Robert Matheau; 115 (left) Photo by James Bland; 121 (top & bottom) Photo courtesy of Tsukasa Fukuoka, T. Kurosawa & Co.; 122 Photo by Jack Rosen; 126 Photo by John Hamill; 136 (left) Photo courtesy of Larry Robinson; 137 Photo courtesy of Larry Robinson; 138 (background) Illustration courtesy of Larry Robinson

Every effort has been made to determine and credit all copyright holders. We apologize for any accidental omissions or errors and will endeavor to amend credits in subsequent editions as appropriate.

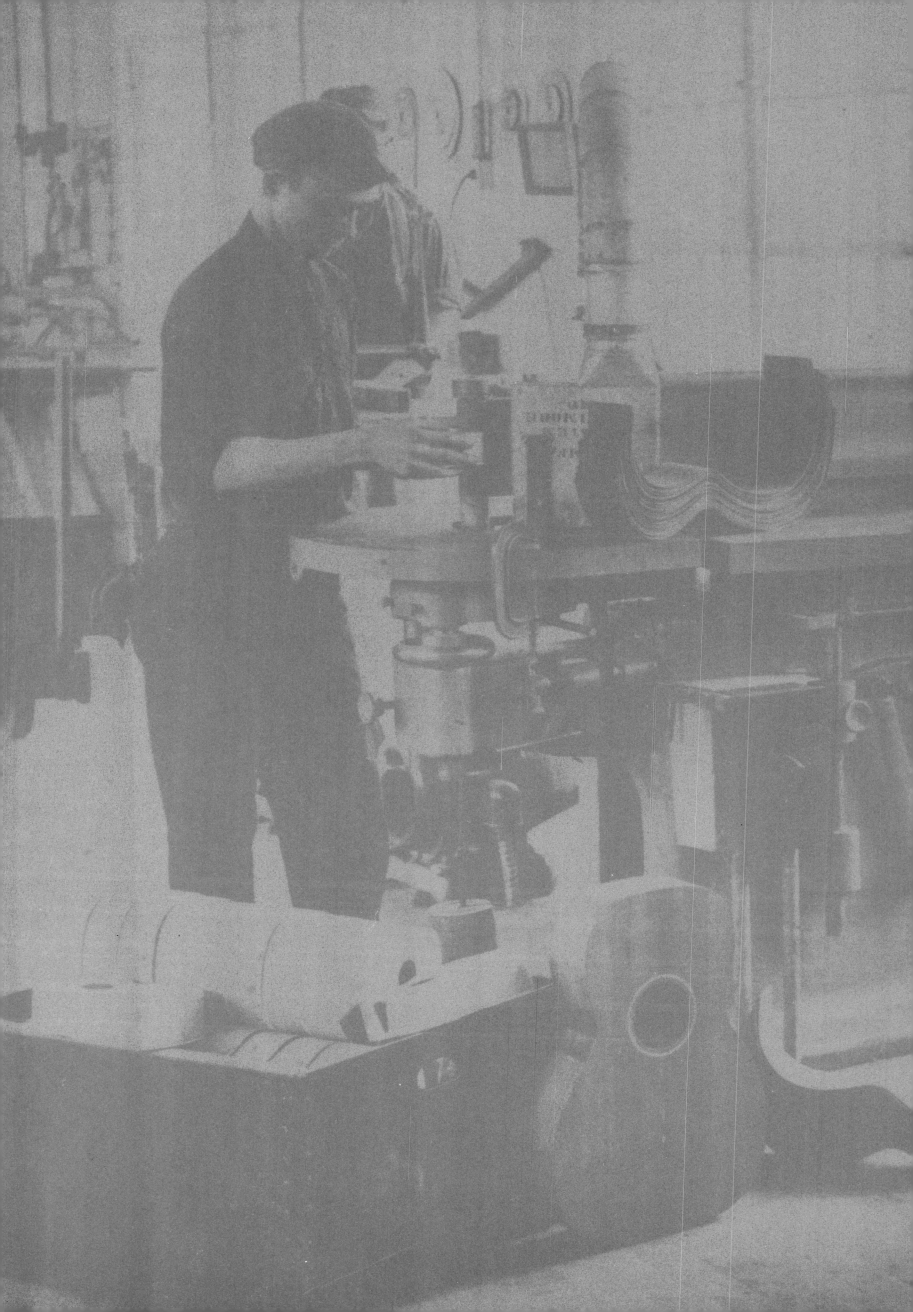